OUTDOOR
DESIGN
PAVING

Clare Matthews

NH
NEW
HOLLAND

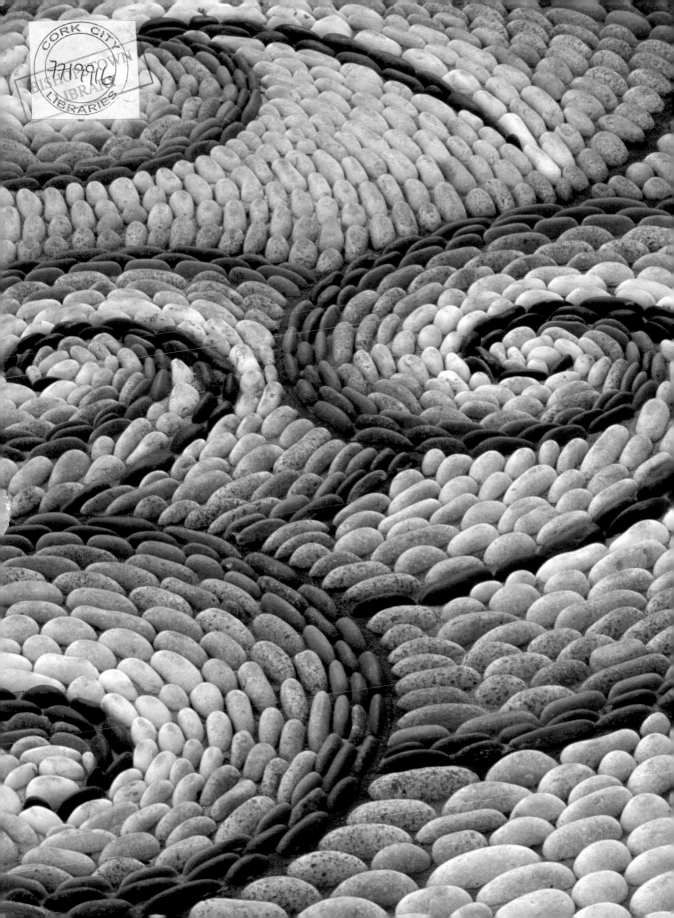

OUTDOOR DESIGN PAVING

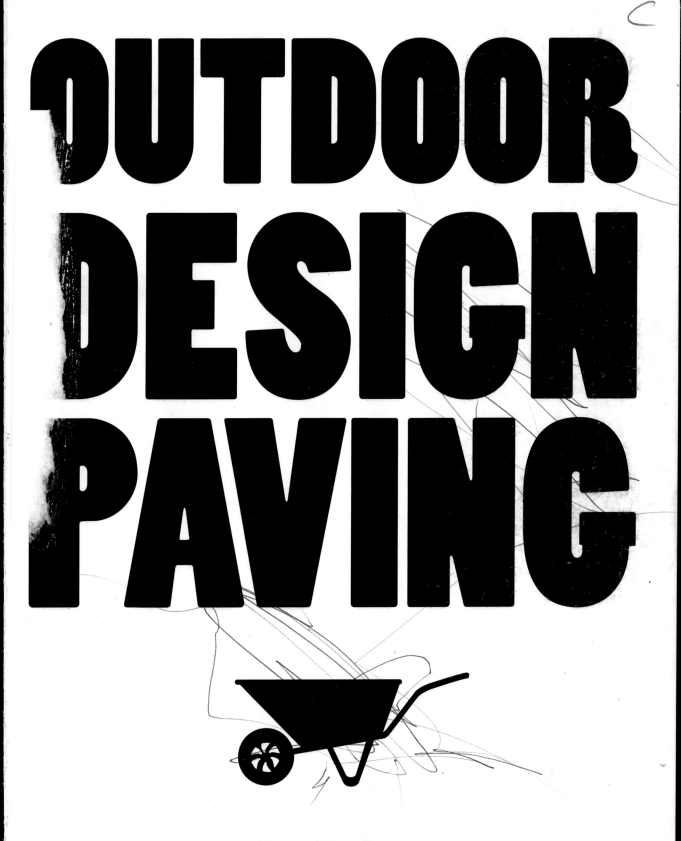

Clare Matthews

First published in 2012 by New Holland Publishers (UK) Ltd
London • Cape Town • Sydney • Auckland

Garfield House
86–88 Edgware Rd
London W2 2EA
United Kingdom

80 McKenzie Street
Cape Town 8001
South Africa

Unit 1
66 Gibbes Street
Chatswood
NSW 2067
Australia

218 Lake Road
Northcote
Auckland
New Zealand

ISBN   978 1 84773 990 2

Publisher: Clare Sayer
Senior Editor: Emma Pattison
Designer: Fiona Andreanelli
Photography: Clive Nichols
Production: Laurence Poos

10 9 8 7 6 5 4 3 2 1

Reproduction by Modern Age Repro House Ltd, Hong Kong
Printed and bound in China by Toppan Leefung Printing Limited

CONTENTS

Introduction

Few gardens are without a paved surface – patios, terraces, paths and driveways – the permanent, immutable hardscaping which give year-round structure to the garden. In many respects paved garden floors prescribe how a garden is used, where to sit, which route to take from one part of the garden to another, and where to eat. So it is well worth investing a good amount of time, energy and imagination in designing these key areas of the garden, searching for inspiration and assessing the absolute best layout for your space.

As a designer, I begin the design process by marking the paved areas onto a plan – perhaps not the exact dimensions at this stage but the best locations for a patio for dining, a small area for relaxing, or whatever my client requires and the net work of paths which with will shape and divide the garden. I then build the rest of the garden around this framework. There are a myriad of ways in which paved surfaces can be elevated from the mundane and given a style and personality that is right for you and your garden. Choosing the right materials, combining materials, building in features, using interesting textures and creating interesting shapes and layouts will all help to produce something individual and special. Though paving is undoubtedly one of the most costly elements of building a new garden, constructing paving with style does not have to be more expensive than something bland.

In this book I describe the process of designing paving, starting from assessing what you really need and what is achievable, through the choice of materials and how to inject style and pizzazz, to how to tackle simple construction projects. The pages are crammed with inspiration for your own projects as well as good solid practical information. Everything you need to confidently plan your own paved area.

PLANNING & DESIGN

Preparing to plan

Most of us want our gardens to be more than just a space to grow plants; we want to inhabit our gardens much as we do our homes, using them for relaxation, entertaining and recreation.

Good paved areas are fundamental to allowing your outdoor space to become a practical, hardworking and irresistible extension to your home, encouraging all kinds of activities out into the open air. Building a well-designed patio can revolutionize the way the garden is used, while paths enhance the garden, adding structure and making navigating the space a simple in all weathers. Building your perfect outdoor room is a great opportunity to enhance family life but it will be a large investment, of both time and money, so it is worth starting at the beginning and working through the design process step-by-step, looking at all the options and firing up your imagination before you begin.

Most gardens will have several areas of paving, patios or terraces to host the many aspects of family life which spill out from the house – ornamental paths which lead one around the garden giving it structure, practical paving for parking cars and more utilitarian paths for moving bicycles, wheelbarrows and dustbins around the garden. These paved surfaces, unchanged by the seasons, are the bones upon which the rest of your garden will hang, they are the spaces dedicated to people rather than plants. Getting them right is fundamental to getting the whole garden right.

A great deal of the hard work in creating marvellous, practical and inspired garden floors goes on well before the building starts, and much of that before a design is even begun. Excited and inspired, it is easy to start drawing shapes on paper and pointing out spaces in the garden, but to start here is to miss out an important part of the design process which may well transform those ideas formulated in haste into something far more dazzling. Before anything else, carefully analyze the nitty gritty of what you really need and really want. If you are merely planning a path. This may be a simple matter, but for a paved terrace in a family garden there are so many ways in which it might be constructed, so many features which might be included, and so many small ways in which the space might be made more beautiful or better tailored to your needs, that if you do not start out with a definite idea about your basic requirements and work through the design process your imagination will not get a chance to do its best work.

Start from the beginning, by developing a clear idea of what the paving is for. Taking time to make a detailed list of requirements can often produce the challenge to inspire greater creativity. Consider not just ordinary everyday use but occasional and extraordinary events; deliberate over extra features you may like to include, such as lighting, an outdoor kitchen or perhaps some moving water. Allow your imagination a free reign and think of ways in which your outdoor space might be made more practical or more pleasurable to use. Consider not just the issues relating to the project in hand but the wider hopes you have for the garden – more privacy, less noise, a better view or even growing your own. Can any of those be tackled or at least partially addressed within this project?

Assessing the potential

There is a strong temptation to slap down a slab of rectangular paving, just about large enough for a table and chairs, outside the back of the house and run paths poker straight from A to B.

This is fine if it is the best spot and is what you want and need, but this can only be determined after you take time to look at the garden with a fresh eye, taking in all it has to offer and less than perfect areas that might be improved. Your assessment should even stray to the landscape beyond the garden – are there any features in the areas beyond the garden which might shape your design? Focal points which might be borrowed or links which might be forged by using similar materials, colours or design styles? Or perhaps you need to distract or discourage the eye from travelling too far?

The most efficient way of recording all of this information is on a scale plan. It need not be to any great standard just an accurate outline of the garden on which details can be marked. Details not only of your impressions but also practical considerations such as services and manhole covers, any overhead wires, changes in level and existing 'must keep' trees and features. If you are planning a small area of paving you may only need to look closely at that portion of the garden, however you may be missing a trick if you focus in too quickly on a particular spot before considering if it really is the best place for your project. Though outside the house is convenient and some paving there is arguably essential, the main seating or dining area may be better placed elsewhere to benefit from a wonderful view, more sun or privacy. There is also the possibility that the area next to the house may prove difficult if there is an extreme change in level. Though sloped areas can be reshaped to produce flat terraces which can be paved, and overcoming this difficulty throws up some interesting design possibilities, moving earth and constructing retaining walls is a costly process. Similarly a network of paths is better laid out when you consider the whole plot.

If you are remodelling the entire garden, taking this broad view comes a little easier than if you are shoehorning new features into an established layout. If you are adding to an existing garden as part of assessing the space, think about how the new addition will work in the existing scheme. Avoid introducing too many new hardscaping materials, consider incorporating at least some of those which are used in the garden already and sticking to a restricted palette of materials to give the garden some unity. To make the new addition successful it needs to sit comfortably in the existing garden, choosing sympathetic styles, materials and colours will all help achieve this.

A change in level should not been seen as a problem but an opportunity to be exploited by incorporating all kinds of features into the design.

Design

Armed with a well thought out list of needs and requirements and a thorough understanding of your plot, you can begin the design process. The simplest way to work is by laying tracing paper over your scale drawing and experimenting by drawing on basic outlines of the new paved areas.

Try different shapes and layouts. You can afford to be bold, replacing or overlapping the tracing paper, transferring successful ideas and scrapping others. This is the time to make mistakes and test ideas as it is only paper you are wasting! Avoid intricate shapes and overcomplicating the outlines. Good hardscaping is invariably simple.

Once the basic shapes of the design are settled, other features which are to be included in your paving project can be slotted in – water features, lighting, pergola, fire pits or outdoor kitchen. It may seem reckless, but trying to work within a budget at this stage is pointless so long as you keep things within the bounds of possibility. It is astounding how imaginative solutions can be found to reduce costs when pressed. The choice of materials alone can significantly affect the cost of an area of paving. Lumieres range widely in cost and these are just a couple of examples of how the same basic design might be built on very different budgets. Using found or recycled materials imaginatively can help to cut costs considerably. Another alternative is to build the project in stages, with a firm idea of the final layout. A patio may be constructed first, say, and paths the following year in the knowledge that the whole scheme will work.

With the layout and features decided, materials can be chosen. By this stage, at least the character, if not the exact palette of materials, are probably already clear in your mind. The multitude of small design details which contribute so much to shaping the character of a paved area can then be worked out, from the way the paving is laid to the width of the joint and the colour of the mortar. If you are employing a landscaper being armed with plenty of detail will help to ensure you get an accurate quotation, and if you are carrying out the work yourself it will avoid ill advised snap decisions made under pressure. Inevitably designs evolve as they are built and necessary changes should not be resisted, but it helps to start with a good set of ideas.

The use of small setts and planting to embellish this natural stone flag paving adds texture, structure and a huge amount of style to this small garden.

Choosing materials

The character of a paved garden floor is to a great extent dictated by the material from which you choose to craft it and how those materials are arranged. Whether you are planning a spacious terrace or a winding garden path, a large part of the impression it makes will be down to the traits of the flags, stones or setts and how they are laid, however you dress the space later. Choosing the right materials to achieve the style and mood you require is key. Imagine a straight length of path in herringbone, hand cut, soft brick; it conjures up a traditional garden, either formal or cottage in style. Imagine a straight length of path in polished, close-butted white granite; it has a contemporary, sleek modern personality.

So, it is easy to see how the material used can influence the final effect and should not strike a discordant note with the mood you hope to create and that of the garden around it. It is easy to be seduced by the appearance of a stone but that alone does not make it perfect for your scheme. If you are redesigning the whole garden then picking out materials is a simple matter but adding to an existing scheme takes more care.

In designing a new garden success often comes from keeping the choice of paving simple, especially if there are different paved areas spread across the garden. Restricting the palette to two or three paving materials, which can be used throughout the garden, perhaps combined in different ways, but essentially repeated throughout. You may have a stone flag terrace with an edging of setts, with a gravel path edged with the same setts, another path in another part of the garden may be completely composed of setts while a small casual seating area might be made

of gravel with a frame of flags. Or you may choose to use the same stone flag but in two different colours or a robust flag stone and brick. Judicious repetition of materials links the garden together, prevents the garden floor from becoming too chaotic and over complicated and gives an interesting designed look. If you are adding to an existing scheme consider using one of the materials already employed in the garden, at least in part, to link the elements together. There will always be an exception to the rule; mosaic paths made of all kinds of bits and pieces for example which add a quirky, decorative twist to the garden or gardens which embrace a flamboyant style to build spaces with exceptional flair and personality, for example The Artist's Garden on pages 122–123.

Above Using two materials can make large areas of paving less dominant as well as more interesting; imagine this scheme in just cobbles. Linking the two, the cobbles are used to edge the stone, giving the paving a common theme.

Combining materials with different textures can provide the opportunity to design some really interesting decorative effects.

The products you choose not only need to sit well within your design, they need to be fit for purpose, provide a surface texture and durability suited to how the area will be used to give a practical, long-lasting garden floor. Most paved surfaces should last for tens of years. (Most frequently, it is the construction rather than the stones which fail as foundations are not robust enough or the pointing is not sound.) The texture of the raw material you use in combination with the width of any mortar joints will dictate how smooth, rough or just plain uneven the finished surface will be. Extremely smooth surfaces, like polished stone, are easy to walk on, and furniture stands without wobbling and wheeled toys and pushchairs will glide across the surface. The downside of this flawless finish is that this type of paving can be slippery when wet. At the opposite end of the scale are uneven warn flags which may have deep dishes and humps and scars of a former life, all of which give a delicious,

comfortable solidity, however furniture may not quite sit level without manoeuvring slightly to find a good spot. Stones described as riven will have an uneven finish, but this should be within reasonable bounds. The different characters of each paving is discussed here but before committing yourself, take stock of the activities to which your surface will play host, how many lumps and bumps in the surface you are willing to live with, and how much 'grip' you need.

Budget will also heavily influence the selection of a material. However, it is not just the cost of the material which will determine the relative cost of the project – different products will require different foundations, different methods of laying (some faster than others) and some may require many units to be cut. If you are planning to complete the work yourself this may be unimportant, the level of skill required may be more relevant, but if you are using a landscaper these factors will influence cost.

When laid well, random flags of natural stone produce a livelier floor than more regimented, regular cut stone.

NATURAL STONE

In the past natural stone was the only choice for long lasting paving and choice was limited to the local stone, but as transportation methods have become more efficient and less expensive stone is shipped far and wide and you can be faced with a choice of stones from all over the world. However environmental concerns are shifting the focus again, and you may like to use locally sourced or reclaimed materials. Using suitable local stone where the architecture is dominated by local stone makes perfect sense aesthetically too; the paved surface will immediately look at home rather than jarring with its surroundings. Otherwise the field is open to select one of the many stones available in one of its many guises.

A product of geological processes taking millennia, each piece of stone is unique and so each pavement or patio it is used to create will be in many respects a one off. Idiosyncrasies in size, colouration and inclusions are part of the charm of natural stone, some even have fossilized marine life strewn across their surface. The lack of uniformity of some stones, however, does make them more challenging and costly to lay than standardized, identical concrete units.

Stones have different properties which dictate how they will perform in the garden. The more porous a stone is the more likely it is to stain. If it is formed in layers, that it is a sedimentary rock, it is more likely to delaminate, meaning layers may split away from the surface as water penetrates and freezes. Not a problem on thick flags as fresh stone is

Some natural stone paving is supplied in a fixed width but a variety of lengths. Cut in this way the paving is far easier to lay than stone, which is completely random in size, as it can be set in bands, yet it still has charm.

revealed beneath the flaky surface. A good mortar joint sealing the edge of the flags can stop water penetration and minimize the problems. Harder rock will show less signs of wear than a softer one, chair scrapes, dropped tools and the odd bump and bash are all part of the normal wear and tear of a paved area, hard stone will show little damage where softer stones will accrue dents and abrasions quickly. Some polished stones can lose their finish. If you want a surface that remains pristine, choose a hard stone.

Some stones are more regular than others, it depends on how they have been cut and finished. Modern cutting tools mean that for some stones at least a good degree of control is achieved. Polished, granite stones for example come with a slick finish, neat straight edges and a reasonably uniform thickness. Sandstone flags, however, are more likely to vary in thickness and have a naturally uneven surface. More expensive sandstone products will have a carefully selected stone, others may range from tile thickness to hefty flags and that at either end of the same stone! The surface finish and regularity will depend on how it has been shaped and then how it is treated. Some stones, such as limestone, form in layers and so can be split along the natural layers in the rock. This produces the slightly uneven surface. Other stone can be sawn to give a regular surface in texture, though the pattern and colours of the stone will still give a natural individuality. Some stones are finished equally well on the sides – sawn sides make them far easier to lay – while others may not be finished on the underside and the edges may be fettled. As a rule, the more that is done to shape and dress the stone, the more expensive it will be. The following pages contain some guidelines as to the character and uses of different stones.

MARBLE

COLOUR	White, cream, pink, green, black, brown, red.
FINISHES	Polished (most usual), honed.
CHARACTER	Polished marble smacks of luxury and quality. Its slick good looks are suited to contemporary schemes and gardens designed for indulgence. Add cooling pools and fountains and lush palms and it is evocative of exotic enclosed courtyards. If you want a grand, opulent, continuous sweep of floor inside and out, polished marble will fit the bill.
POTENTIAL PROBLEMS	Marble may stain, particularly if the polished surface has been damaged through wear, chemical cleaners, weathering or pollution. This is probably the least hardy paving stone and so will easily be damaged, marring its polished good looks.

Marble can have a marvellously opulent and exotic appeal. Flanked by palms this elegant pool is surrounded by a polished marble frame and is easily traversed on the glossy stepping stones set just above the water's surface.

Slate can be a plain stone or be marked with dramatic patterns which contrast strongly with the main colour of the stone.

SLATE

COLOUR	Silver-grey, grey, blue, brown, green and black.
FINISHES	An uneven riven texture, the degree of unevenness will vary from product to product. Look at a number of stones from the supplier to gauge how uneven the finish will be as well as referring to the specification. In general, less expensive products will tend to be more uneven. Slate is sometimes polished and honed to give a more refined finish.
CHARACTER	Essentially slate is very versatile and can be acquired in a wide range of sizes up to the largest flags. The personality of the stone varies greatly with the colour and finish. Slate is one of the flags that can be used successfully to make a continuous floor flowing from the outside in.
POTENTIAL PROBLEMS	Not as hard as limestone or granite, slate is nevertheless very durable. The main problem is likely to be with staining with oily substances, though the degree to which this is a problem will depend on the particular slate as some are more porous than others. Applying a sealant can ease this problem. Slate may also delaminate.

Slightly riven, grey slate flags provide the perfect contrast to shinning bright white furniture and rendered walls.

GRANITE

COLOUR

Most granite is speckled, made up of granules of different colours and many different colours are possible, from white through pinks and greens to blacks. Many types of granite will have inclusions which may produce a subtle sparkle when caught by the sun.

FINISHES

Granite paving is sold in an array of finishes and shapes from rough, chunky setts to smooth slabs with a highly polished finish.

CHARACTER

The stone is very strong and hard. Setts are rough, rugged-looking and hardwearing. They make tough edging for paths or areas of gravel and are an interesting accent material where pattern and texture are needed. Polished with machine cut edges, the stone is transformed, the patterns within the stone are enhanced and it has a clean, crisp character suited to urban, contemporary projects where a stone which is one step removed from the natural is required. Generally polished granite is available as 30 x 30 cm (12 x 12 in) stones.

POTENTIAL PROBLEMS

In its rough state it is incredibly durable and age will not adversely affect its looks. The surface of polished stones however can be chipped, but normal use should not cause a problem.

Below Ice white, sawn granite setts provide a crisp, bright flooring for this enclosed and minimal courtyard garden. The smooth black marble pebbles are just enough to frame the paving providing definition, otherwise the white flooring would merge seamlessly with the white wall.

Below Setts can be combined with other materials to produce highly textured garden floors – here the joints in the sett floor are filled with gravel. The muted colours and small variations spread across the entire surface make for a comfortable, easy going feel.

When polished to a mirror -like shine, granite becomes glossy and glamorous.

SANDSTONE

COLOUR	White, green, grey, yellow and brown.
FINISHES	Textured, riven, polished and honed.
CHARACTER	The colour and the texture of the stone go a long way to determine its character. It is generally available in large flags to small 10 x 10 cm (4 x 4 in) setts.
POTENTIAL PROBLEMS	This is a hard stone, however, as it is very absorbent it can be prone to staining, particularly with grease. I have seen sandstone laid using the five spot method where the 'spots' were often clearly visible on the surface: the fault of the laying, not the stone. As it so absorbent it can tend to look a little grubby with age. May delaminate.

LIMESTONE

COLOUR	Pale shades with flecks and patterns caused by inclusions. Solid blacks, browns and greys are available.
CHARACTER	The character of limestone varies considerably, there is probably a limestone suited to most projects.
POTENTIAL PROBLEMS	Though each source will produce stones with a different nature, overall limestone is not as hard as granite or sandstone but harder than marble. It is liable to stain and like sandstone is highly absorbent. Sealers can be used to solve this problem.

THINGS TO CONSIDER

Natural stone invariably comes at a premium and laying these stones is more exacting and time consuming because of the potential for quirks in shape, size and thickness, and the possibility of staining with mortar during the pointing process. If you are planning to employ a landscaper check they are familiar with the stone you wish to use. Laying large uneven flags in particular is an exacting task, requiring skill, patience and more than a little muscle.

For patios and garden paths for light traffic, thinner stones are acceptable, though they will require the support of a full bed of mortar. Stones 7–15 cm (2¾–6 in) will support very light slow vehicular traffic. It is always as well to ask your supplier about the capabilities of the stone he supplies and the recommended method of laying. This not only ensures you have the right stone for the job it also means you will be in the best position possible if faults arise.

Choosing the colour of stone can be challenging, and most ranges will come in a choice of colour. The difficulty comes in imagining the effect of a large expanse of one stone when confronted with a sample or just a few flags. Try to look at images of finished projects if possible. With dark stones, deep greens, brown and blacks, will a large area appear too solid and dominant? If the stone is for a terrace near the house it may darken the aspect from the windows. Equally a large sweep of very light paving may dominate as it leaps out of its surroundings, with a dazzling brightness. In dark stone a space will tend to look smaller, while lighter stones have the opposite effect. Some natural stones have dramatic sweeping patterns across their surface. These may look appealing on one stone but how will the patio look with a random spread of swoops,

Vast stone flags have a fantastic solidity and permanence about them but they are very heavy and very difficult to manoeuvre. Vacuum slab lifters can be useful, though they require two people to operate them and have a weight limit.

curves and meanders fragmented across the surface? Plain stones present other problems; a featureless, immaculate black surface looks stunning but just a few stray leaves will really stand out. The final point to check when thinking about colour is how does the stone look when rained upon – in some parts of the world you can spend many months of the year looking out at a wet terrace. Most stones will darken considerably once wet and can become very dull and dismal looking, while with other stones colours and patterns are intensified.

Laying a terrace in natural stone is a costly business and if you hope to be enjoying it for years to come without tiring of it, avoiding the latest or novelty stone and plumping for a material with a timeless appeal is common sense.

LOOSE MATERIALS

Gravel, slate, crushed stone and bark chip can all be used to create garden floors; though not strictly paving all can be used to create paths, seating and dining areas and drives. The big advantage of loose materials is cost, not only are they relatively inexpensive to buy, they are quick and simple to put down and, depending on how they are being used, may need little ground work. Using some loose material as part of a scheme can be a good way to stretch a budget. A terrace leading onto a gravel area for less formal activity for example can work well, giving a larger area for a far less investment in terms of time and materials. Most commonly loose paving materials are used on paths, drives and parking areas where a practical all weather surface is required but as these areas are often large other types of paving may be prohibitively expensive. One of the advantages of loose materials set on a permeable base is water drains quickly from the surface.

Unfortunately gravel and other loose materials are less successful on drives or areas with a very steep gradient. It is impossible to give an exact gradient beyond which it is impractical to use gravel, to some extend gravel beds in and packs down making the surface more stable, though gravel which is constantly raked and primped does not form such a stable surface as that which is left to lock together. Vehicles will tend to move the gravel down the slope and if drainage is poor in torrential rain the gravel may wash down the incline forming interesting banks and spits on the way. There are ways to limit the movement, by incorporating bands of setts or bricks into the design, however the gravel then builds up against the barrier. I owned a gravel drive on a hill and about once a year, after heavy storms, I had to spend some time hauling the gravel from the bottom of the drive back up to the top, a price I was happy to pay for a crisp gravel drive.

Getting the thickness of the loose material right is key, too thin and you will be forever covering 'bald' patches where the base is showing through, too thick and walking becomes hard work, like walking up a pebble beach. In general a wearing course of 5–7.5 cm (2–3 in) when first laid should do the trick, this will compact with use. If security is a concern loose materials (with the exception of woodchips) are a good choice, they are very noisy, driving and walking produces a loud and distinctive 'crunch'. For this reason gravel is a good material for paths around the sides of the house.

Above Perhaps not the most practical of paths but certainly incredibly colourful, crushed glass looks wonderful but is really only suited to the least hardworking paths.

Patios, terraces and courtyards with a gravel floor tend to look more relaxed and effortless than those with a base of solid paving.

GRAVEL

From a design point of view not all gravels are equal; they vary considerably in colour and the shape of the individual stones, which in turn determines how a surface clothed with them will look. Angular gravels are less welcoming than softer rounded gravel. Crushed stone is for me the least appealing, its sharp edges and manufactured look smacks of fakery and it never looks as welcoming as natural products. Products which have been coloured or dyed can also look a little awkward unless used in the right setting. In general gravel is a fairly quiet, neutral surface, that is to say it does not have a striking character and so is the perfect foil for plants or other paving stones with more personality.

Most types of gravel will be available a in two or three sizes, these may be quoted as a range, a minimum and maximum size of stones in the mix or as a single figure which is an approximate or average size of all the individual stones. Gravels are usually available from 6–20 mm (¼–¾ in), larger sizes may be available, up to 40 mm (1½ in) but these chunky stones are best used as a decorative mulch as stones over 20 mm (¾ in) are not comfortable to walk on. The size of gravel you choose is to some extent a matter of personal preference. Small stones are lighter, travel more and tend to get stuck in the tread of tyres and shoes. They do, however, produce a very crisp, neat surface which appears softer and smoother than that made by large stones. Larger

stones are more durable, better suited to vehicular traffic but they produce a rather more lumpy finish. In general 6–10 mm (¼–½ in) stones are suited to paths and 10–18 mm (½–¾ in) for drives, but there are no hard and fast rules.

An alternative to loose gravel is gravel bound in a clay matrix: this is known as hoggin or bound gravel. These products vary in consistency but basically they are laid on a foundation of compacted scalping and compacted with a vibrating roller and then compacted with a wet roller so the clay and the stone bind together to form a stable surface. The durability of the final wearing course is down to how well it is laid and this is probably a task best left to the professionals.

Above left Punctured by hunks of natural stone, gravel's immensely mutable character adapts perfectly to an informal style.

Above top Gravel is the perfect collaborator for loose, reckless planting and weather-beaten wood.

Above bottom Including a gravel area alongside a patch of solid paving adds interest to the scheme, stretches the budget and provides the opportunity to plant through the gravel.

WOOD CHIPPINGS

Flakes and slivers of wood sold as wood chips, make a reasonable loose paving in informal and wood land areas. They are inexpensive and simple to lay. The downside is they can be slippery and slimy when wet and crispy and sharp when dry. Overtime they will begin to rot and will undoubtedly need topping up each year or two. Birds also delight in sorting through looking for a quick snack and in the process spread the chips far and wide. Dyed bark chips are sometimes available, these are fun but in my experience they soon fade losing their punchy colours. Natural wood chips look most at home in a sylvan setting, or where a short-term quick fix is needed.

Above right A bench set in a secluded corner of the garden does not need a tranche of hard paving to stand upon – a covering of woodchip will be enough to keep the weeds down and allow safe passage to the bench in good weather.

Above left In this jungle-style garden packed with leafy green plants, woodchip is a sympathetic choice of materials for paths and seating area floors.

SLATE

In soft shades of plum, green, blue and silver grey, which intensify when it is wet, a layer of slate mulch makes a richly coloured and interesting garden surface. The flat shards of slate produce a completely different texture to that of gravel slate demands far more attention and can look heavy over large areas. Its relatively high cost means it is usually used only on paths which are more decorative than practical.

The large irregular shards of blue slate mulch.

CONCRETE FLAGS

There are many advantages to choosing a manmade paving stone. They are made to be convenient to lay: They are regular sizes, thicknesses and shapes, they are predictable in colour and finish and will behave as expected when cut. Some concrete stones do not masquerade as natural stone, these are either the very robust, functional stones or there are those that revel in being artificial, using colour and texture to create something fantastic and appealing in its own right. There is an array of interesting, well-crafted products designed with an eye to dressing a contemporary garden floor with striking patterns and exciting effects. However, there are plenty of manmade flags which imitate stone and some do this incredibly well, especially once they have been down a while and seen a little wear, which dulls the bright newness of the surface. Then the best manmade stones can easily be mistaken for the real thing.

Crushed natural stone or other aggregate is sometimes used to make up the body of the stone, held in a cement-based matrix. The surface of these stones is brushed away to reveal the aggregate and some are polished to give a spectacular finish. Others are known as reconstituted stone; natural stone is ground and mixed with the cement so the stones take their colour from the ground stone. Moulded to replicate natural stone these can be very convincing.

As these are all manufactured products they are made to certain standards and will be of known strength so it makes sense to check the product you are considering is suited to your project and how it should be laid, this advice is likely to vary depending whether they will take foot traffic or vehicular traffic.

Pillow-like, the flags of this staggeringly tactile concrete design produce a path which seems to sway from side to side.

The cost of manmade products, as might be expected, is in general less than that of similar-sized natural stones, though there is definite overlap where the least expensive natural products can seem more cost effective than the most costly man made products. The advice given for natural stone on choosing colour and texture apply equally to concrete flags.

PEBBLE MOSAIC

Closely packed pebbles form a surprisingly even surface. Arranged neatly the pebbles in a pebble mosaic almost have a nap – like fur or velvet which can be used to direct the eye and make subtle and interesting patterns. Curving and spiralling designs can almost look as if they are flowing over the surface, while alternating squares or pebbles orientated in one direction and then another produces a more static design. Slate, shards of terracotta pot, glass marbles and numerous other materials can be incorporated into the design. The pebbles must be tightly packed for the best effect and a generous bedding of mortar which comes at least half to three quarters of the way up the pebbles will ensure the resulting surface not only looks good but will last for years.

Although creating a pebble mosaic is a simple process, it is very time-consuming but if you want a truly unique garden floor then pebble mosaic offers the opportunity to construct something special, reflecting your own taste and style. Pebbles are available in a plethora of colours and as the pebbles can be small, fairly intricate patterns can be executed with pebbles of contrasting colours, or more subtly by manipulating their direction. As the process is time consuming pebble mosaics surfaces tend to small, a tiny patio for a table for two, panels inset in other paving to add a touch of spice or fabulously decorative stretches of path in prominent areas of the garden. There is of course no reason why larger projects are not possible, in fact the process becomes quite relaxing as you focus attention on placing one small pebble at a time to produce the bigger picture.

The character of the mosaic depends on the pebbles and the design and so it is possible to design something to fit in with any style of garden, a quaint cottage garden to formal grandeur the right pebble mosaic would sit happily in each. Sketch out a design on paper, a simple scale drawing will help ensure your proposed design or pattern will fit within the space available.

A striking, bold monochrome design serves to add interest and texture to the garden floor and garner more attention for the arbour beyond.

An elegant
monochrome
pebble grid has
no direction,
producing a
relaxing static
space.

RANDOM STONE PAVING

Done well random paving, also known as crazy paving, can look fantastic, done badly it looks rather less appealing. The term is used to describe a paved surface made up of randomly shaped pieces of stone or slab. It is an excellent way of using pieces of natural stone, which cannot be transformed into regular flags and even recycling old or damaged paving which can be deliberately broken to create the pieces. The trick is to ensure it looks like a design choice rather than an expedient measure, even if it is! In general too many small pieces make a surface that looks too chaotic, especially over a large area as the web of mortar joints dominates. Extra large stones, carefully arranged, have a far calmer surface. Whatever the nature and size of the stones the key to a achieving a pleasing finish is taking the time to arrange the stones so there is some kind of fit between them rather than relying on wide mortar joints to overcome the lumps and bumps in the shapes of the stones. Too little effort to match stones results in a surface in which you notice the mortar joints before the stones. Extra wide mortar joints will also make the paving more likely to fail and suggests this is a quick fix to use up spare materials.

The jigsaw of stones has an inherent informality, the edges can be left jagged, with no effort to contrive a straight edge, this works well where the paving flows into an area of planting or gravel. Alternatively a crisper finish is to be had by cutting the edge stones so the paving ends neatly. If you really want a tidy finish, which gives a deliberate, tailored look to the area contain the random paving within a frame of brick, setts or stone flags.

A random stone surface is sometimes the best choice for the job, leisurely descending through naturalistic planting. A more regimented surface may be too much of an intrusion.

BRICK

Brick is a very versatile paving material, which looks at home in many types of garden depending on how it is used. As bricks are small and have an almost 'go with anything' character as there are so many to choose from they are an ideal choice for a second paving material alongside natural stone flags for example, they make good frames, edges and in fills. The trick is choosing the right brick. If the house is built of brick then to keep things simple and forge a strong bond between house and garden use the same brick as the house. There are hundreds of types of bricks, but a good supplier should have a fair sized library of sample bricks to compare with your own. With older properties a local brick will often prevail and so the search may be simpler or even involve a trip to a reclamation yard.

As the brick is a small unit of paving it tends to look better in smaller spaces if it is used to produce an expanse of paving as it can look too busy, as the frequent mortar joints dominate the surface and rather too heavy. It is far more suited to small courtyards and cottage gardens if it is to be used as a main paving material. Most bricks are not designed to be used as paving, the wear and tear and the effects of the weather are quite different from those endured by a vertical wall, so these bricks will quite reasonably age quickly. They may crack, flake and wear lending them a well-used, individual character. Depending on your taste this may be desirable or disappointing. Personally I prefer the softer look and have even used reclaimed bricks to achieve an instant worn in look. Some bricks are more durable than others; your supplier should be able to advise you about the qualities of individual bricks. Engineering bricks are the most durable bricks, these are commonly used to cap walls as well as to form steps and in paving. Unfortunately, however, these

bricks are more expensive than run of the mill bricks. Originally used in stables, stable paviours are another hardwearing brick, usually in blue grey their surface is divided into squares, rather like a bar of chocolate. The chamfered edges of the brick mean that although they are usually laid butt-jointed, without a mortar joint, they appear to have one. Diamond paviours have a diamond pattern inscribed on its surface, designed to give good grip. Both of these paviours make an excellent choice for decorative detailing, particularly in traditional schemes.

The straightforward rectangular brick can be conjured into an array of patterns, called bonds. The bond you choose will influence the look and the direction of the surface. Stack bond is the simplest, followed by running or stretcher bond. Both are strongly directional, pulling the eye quickly along their surface or slowing it down and stretching spaces or compacting them, depending upon which way the prominent lines in the surface are orientated. Running bond, where the long side of the brick is orientated with the direction of the path, is the best choice for gently curved paths, the frequency of the joints mean curves are easy to create and the lines of the pattern emphasize the arcs and swoops of the path. Straight paths in running bond will appear longer than they are in reality. Stretcher bond, where the long side of the brick runs across the path, will make a slower path which appears wider than a path of the same dimensions in running bond. Basket weave, where two or three bricks are placed side by side to form a square and two or three bricks are placed next to them at 90° and so on, especially where three bricks on edge are used to form the bond rather than two bricks flat is a very fussy pattern but static. Herringbone is arguably less busy and can have a pull on the eye depending upon how it is orientated. With all of these patterns brick can be laid on edge or flat.

TERRACOTTA

Soft, warm and smooth underfoot terracotta, meaning 'baked earth', carries with it all the heat of the sun-baked Mediterranean. Available in a range of colours from rich orangey brown to paler pinky beige terracotta tiles are only produced in small sizes, so like brick they are best used in smaller spaces as they produce a very busy floor. Terracotta is one of the surfaces which work equally well inside as out however of the vast numbers of tiles available only some are frost proof. As the tiles are thinner and less robust than other paving it is important that they be laid on the correct foundation to give them adequate support. Suited to paths, terraces and steps these tiles would be unsuited to commercial projects or areas which are used by vehicles.

Opposite top A shift of 45° in the direction the bricks are laid clearly distinguishes the hurried path from the small relaxed seating area.

Opposite bottom Flanked by Tulipa 'Ballerina', this generous herringbone brick path has a moderate directional pull.

Bottom left The weathered terracotta floor of this terrace works perfectly with the vibrant colour and decorative style of this terrace. The floor has been enhanced by a arranging the tiles to form a patterned border at its edge.

Bottom right Immediately redolent of the Mediterranean, soft, muted terracotta tiles and worn terracotta jar make perfect partners.

EDGING

Edging is one of those small details, often an afterthought in the design process which can have a dramatic impact on a design. Whether it is to contain a loose paving material or to form a frame around a stretch of solid paving including a strong edging detail in a design always makes for a neater more finished look. Drawing attention to the edges, the places where different elements which make up the garden meet emphasizes the shapes they form. It is the equivalent of highlighting the outline of the shapes you have drawn on your plan so they might be better appreciated. There is a careful balance to be struck, however, as too bold or strong an edging might actually distract from the rest of the design. A well chosen or subtle edging will keep things neat and orderly. Sometimes in an expanse of paving a self edging is enough, a boarder of the same type of stone but in a different size or shape is just enough to frame the space.

Edging to retain a loose material like gravel for example has a practical function too, it should be high enough the hold back the gravel as it is scuffed and moves around the path by feet or tyres and robust enough to stand occasionally being trodden on or even driven over if that is likely. There is plenty of off-the-peg edging, from the plain to the decorative, though brick or setts are a common choice. Gravel board screwed to stakes driven into the ground is often used as it is quick, easy and inexpensive. This is perhaps the least obtrusive edging, though even this can be jazzed up with a daub of brightly coloured wood stain. Improvised edging can be equally successful and presents the opportunity to add you own style to the garden, particularly it does not need to withstand the pressures of heavy traffic. Such edging might merely be pushed into the soil and achieve enough strength to do the job whereas on much used paths and drives edging should be firmly fixed into place with concrete.

Above left Hunks of local rock nestled into the soil ably hold back this Cotswold gravel, though an informal edging they have been carefully orientated to flow along the edge of the bed. This also obviously makes the material go further.

Above middle Edgings not only keep the gravel out of the soil but also the plants from lolling onto the gravel. A sweep of fragrant lavender 'Ashdown Forest' is partially restrained by bricks set at an angle, one against another.

Above right Slightly haphazard but completely charming and in tune with the frilly planting behind them these granite setts have quite a different character to the same material bound into neat columns and rows by mortar.

RECLAIMED

Flags, bricks, edging and setts will often keep their appeal far longer than the structures they are used to create. In fact on many materials the patina of wear makes transforms them into something which immediately looks as if it belongs. These materials are softer, worn in not worn out, with all the sharp edges and bright newness gone. Flags worn smooth by hundreds of years of passing feet, or bricks with crumbled edges which has once formed part of a wall or home will not appeal to everyone or be right for every scheme but they can be a cost effective way of getting good quality materials.

There are of course many pitfalls to buying reclaimed material. The quality, the amount of wear or damage will not be consistent across the material, unscrupulous dealers might hide very damaged, unusable materials in the middle of pallets rather than rejecting them. Only the most attractive being on display. With very old flags the sizes and thickness varies considerably so never buy them by weight as you may find a few very large, very thick stones making up the bulk of the weight so you will cover very little area. If possible always buy flags by area. The need to find a reliable supplier is perhaps more of an imperative than with reclaimed goods. It is important to look at materials carefully, do not be afraid of inspecting what is on offer thoroughly. If you buy online be onsite to inspect the goods when they arrive.

When a house changes hands it is not unknown for paving which is just a few years old to be lifted and replaced, though this is not as aged as other reclaimed materials it can be reused if lifted carefully. All mortar should be knocked off and the surface freshened up with a pressure washer.

Some very successful designs start with being confronted by a pile of stones or bricks too good to pass up. The unpredictable and limited supply of these materials often leads to very creative and imaginative solutions combining materials to make unique garden floors.

Above Stout, reclaimed granite curbs make paving which looks as though it will last for centuries. The chips and wear they have accrued in their former life and the process of demolition only add to their charms. In fact this is the third time they have been used as I bought them from the crew demolishing a car park, their second employ, before that they were used to edge paths.

Joints & pointing

It may seem a little obsessive to devote time and energy to pointing the mortar joints between units of paving, but the pointing is the mesh that holds the whole scheme together.

Good pointing should go unnoticed but bad pointing will spoil the most well designed space or the most expensive stone. Pointing should not only be aesthetically pleasing it serves an important practical role in sealing the paviours or flags together and preventing the ingress of water which would eventually damage the foundations and in some cases the stones themselves.

In the normal course of events the colour of mortar is dictated by the mix of sand and cement. This, however, can be varied slightly by using white cement or different sands or more for more dramatic colours special pigments can be added to the mix. In most situations mortar should be effectively invisible, though some interesting and outlandish effects can be achieved by switching the emphasis from paving to joints by using bright colours.

Getting the width of the joint between stones or bricks just right is also important, too wide or too narrow can give equally disappointing results. There is an element of personal taste here but in general large flags will take wider mortar joints than smaller paving units like terracotta tile or brick, joints are likely to be between 10–20 mm (½–¾ in). If you are laying the stones yourself then you can actually layout a few stones, experimenting with the width of the joints. If you are employing a landscaper it is worth confirming you share the same idea about how your paving should be laid.

Though mortar joints should be of a uniform width there are occasions when the joints have to be tweaked a little to get an arrangement which looks right, though it may not be entirely accurate. Crisp square stones demand accurate, regular, crisp joints to look good, irregular, reclaimed or random paving may need joints of varying sizes to achieve a pattern which looks right. This cannot be calculated as it is purely a matter of aesthetics, sections of paving have to be laid with a more or less regular joint width and then these joints can be gently altered so though the gaps may be irregular, there is the minimum difference possible across the whole stretch of paving and it looks right.

It is also worth paying some attention to the depth of the finished joint, pointing is finished with a pointing iron (see page 97) or an improvised pointing iron, a length of hose for example. If the joint is left too deep it will collect water and debris making sweeping the paving a far harder task than it need be. Joints need not be mortar filled, they could be crammed with gravel, plants, pebbles pushed into the mortar or the paving may be butt jointed, with stones or bricks placed tightly together. Each will give a different twist to the way the paving looks.

Clockwise from top Using loose gravel or pea shingle to fill joints looks appealing but the gravel will inevitably hop out of the joints; An enlarged joint holds a string of pebbles, adding texture and pattern; Well-finished joints produce a tidy surface even in random stone paving.

Colour & texture

Though forming the skeleton on which the rest of the garden hangs, the 'good bones' which give structure and carry the garden through the unforgiving winter months when there is little of interest in the garden, paving is seldom the star.

It is the venue for activities dressed with furniture and pots, a foil to show off plants, the all weather surfaces which lead the visitor around the garden or make passage to the compost heap possible in all weathers. However, the details of the paved surface, not just the shape and position, but colour, texture and pattern dramatically affects how the paving is used and the charm of the garden.

The texture of the paving has an effect on the speed at which it is traversed, smooth polished stones will encourage passage at speed, a rough, riven texture will slow progress slightly, very uneven rock or loose materials are crossed more slowly still. Very rugged, informal garden floors littered with plants, the lumpy texture of reclaimed cobbles or awkwardly placed stepping stones, make progress slower still. Obviously the will of the person walking has an effect they may dawdle or be in a hurry irrespective of the surface but using a smooth surface on a short, straight, narrow path will not encourage a relaxing pace and so the atmosphere of the garden is, in part at least, shaped.

The colour of the paving can be used to manipulate light and space. Pale coloured paving reflects more light than darker stones, in shady, dull corners pale stones can be used to brighten the area. This is especially useful where the paving is set outside the north facing elevation of a house, here a dark paving would appear to rob the windows of light, whereas pale stone will bounce back all the light available, brightening the rooms. The same area of light stone will also appear larger than dark stone or brick, which may also be used to advantage in the design process. Large areas of brick and dark paving can appear leaden and dominating, though the brightness of white limestone for example can also lead it to dominate, drawing the eye. Very pale stone can appear stark and less than comfortable. It is a question of which effect will best suit your location, intention and design. Neutral tones provide the safest option, if you are unsure, stay firmly in the middle ground. Warm, pale, earthy tones produce paved surfaces which are welcoming, comfortable and easy to live with.

A beautiful combination of smooth rocks and pebbles encourage a slow and careful pace.

Patios, courtyards & terraces

Originally inspired by the courtyards of Persia and Moorish Spain, the patio is a permanent outdoor space devoted not to gardening but to people.

Arranged for enjoying life outdoors, patios can be equipped for dining, relaxing, play and entertaining. The patio is an extension of the house, where family activity can spill out into the open air whenever the weather allows, a bridge between inside and out. In designing the perfect patio for your needs there is a choice to be made as to how far it is part of the garden and how much it is an extension of the house. As the boundaries blur, interior design and garden design can come together to produce a convincing cocktail of features to transform the way you live outdoors. Essential to this versatile space planned for people not for plants is an enduring paved floor.

Patio, courtyard and terrace are in modern terms different spaces, patio is an area of paving normally next to the back of the house, though this does not have to be the case. A courtyard is surrounded by buildings or walls and the terrace though used to describe a level area carved into a slope is strictly speaking a paved area or patio with a low surround. All have a paved surface and in most respects factors affecting their design are the same.

With thought and planning the paved element of your garden should prove to be a stylish hardworking outdoor space as well used and valued as any other room in the house. Looking at books and magazines is an excellent source of inspiration but it is important not to be seduced by stunning designs or extremes of fashion which do not match your needs.

A plan view shows how skilfully this sleek contemporary space devoted to relaxation has been planned. The bulky, comfortable furniture fits the generous space perfectly, with plenty of room for moving between the chairs to the garden beyond.

SHAPE, SIZE & LOCATION

The survey of the opportunities your site has to offer and your list of needs, should give you plenty of information to shape ideas about the location and size of your patio. Instinctively most opt for the area next to the house, understandably so, as this is the most convenient area if food, plates and all the paraphernalia essential to alfresco cooking and dining are to carried out. However, it may be that another location makes far more sense. It may afford more privacy, enjoy the sun for more of the day or look out over an exceptional view. In larger gardens it may be feasible to have two terraces one which enjoys the sun in the morning one in the evening and at the peak of the summer the cooler terrace can be used for dining in the day too. If the main patio or terrace is to be sited away from the house then it should be furnished with stout, easily negotiable paths along which people and things can be transported easily.

Softened with copious planting in large troughs, the walls of this tiny courtyard provide shelter and privacy with just enough room for a large dining table at its centre.

Choosing the right size for the patio is a balancing act, it needs to be in scale with the house and surroundings, provide enough space for all the activities it will host and stay within budget. For those who frequently entertain in lavish style the size of the paved surface should be as generous as space and budgets allow. In small yards a completely paved surface with just beds left for planting is a practical solution. In other situations a small private area for quiet relaxation and a table for two might be all that is required. Consider how many people will normally be dining, how often you intend to entertain and how many you might need to accommodate then. Would it be beneficial to include space for relaxation with less formal furniture, steamer chairs, benches or outdoor sofas and low tables? Will there be room for children to play?

How the patio is framed, how it is woven into the fabric of the garden will have an impact on how large and dominant it appears, clever planting both on and around the area can help bed the paving into the garden disguising an oversized patio.

Drawing furniture and indicating anticipated walkways through the patio on your scale plan will help make decisions about the ideal size. Using string or marking out spray to rough out the area in the garden will give an idea of how it will sit in the garden.

The shape of the terrace will be, at least in part, dictated by its location. Overly complicated, fussy shapes are not only challenging to construct they are seldom as successful as bolder, simpler designs. Often simply adding a smooth arc at the front of the terrace if it is next to the house or chopping off corners at 45° is just enough. If you plan to have different areas of activity the shape can evolve around these a deeper area for dining tapering to a less lavish space for more relaxed seating. If the patio extends around the corner of the house consider shaping the corner to save materials and labour. Circular areas are often successful where the patio is cut loose from the house, furnished with a circular table and nestled in a sweep of planting these are naturally static, inward looking spaces perfect for relaxation.

A patio can be a great device for unifying a house that has been extended, a purposeful shape which will draw the different elements of the house together. In general straight sided shapes suit a formal garden, whereas bold swooping, organic shapes produce a more laid-back space.

FURNITURE

A lacklustre patio can be revitalized by the right furniture. In fact if you enjoy change and the process of creation then there is a good solid argument for building a good quality patio devoid of features, a blank canvas which can be dressed and restyled in a myriad of different ways, each year if needed. A change of furniture, cushions, pots and planting can completely transform a space say from traditional formal dining area to laid-back Mediterranean living space or given a restrained minimal look. If this appeals then select a good-quality but neutral paving and arrange it in a simple pattern and leave it there. Steer clear of built in features and focal points and use the art of the decorator to leave your mark, imbuing the patio with some pizzazz and personality.

Furniture will have a huge impact on the appeal of the finished patio. Not just on how it looks but how restful it is to use. There are a myriad of styles of garden furniture available but not all are comfortable, if you want diner guests to linger testing chairs and loungers is essential! Ideally choosing furniture should be part of the design process, its character should fit in with the style you are hoping to achieve and be generous enough to seat the right number of people. It also needs to fit on your patio. Drawing it onto the proposed scaled layout will ensure there is space for everything. Remember to allow space for people to move around as well as planters, barbecues, heaters and all the other bits and pieces which might usefully find their way onto the terrace.

The only other factor to consider is storage. The easiest option is to choose furniture which will survive outdoors all year round, not just because it is easier than stowing things away for winter but because looking out onto a denuded patio is just a little sad. If you do select some items which need

winter protection covers are an option, but these are seldom a pleasure to look at, otherwise ensure you have enough shed space to cope.

Wood is natural and inviting. Wooden furniture however will require some maintenance if it is to keep a fresh appearance, oils and preservatives can be applied to protect the wood and improve its colour. This might need to be done every year. The alternative is to allow wood to age, most become a soft silver grey, which suits some more organic, relaxed schemes perfectly. Inexpensive soft wood furniture can be perked up with a coat of paint or opaque wood stain. Stone furniture is heavy and expensive but should last forever. Metal furniture forged from stainless steel and polished metals has a contemporary edge, whereas wrought and cast iron have a traditional character. Synthetic rattan and wicker furniture are some of the most comfortable available and some manufacturers promise UV

stability and long life even when left outside all year round. Other materials like bamboo are seldom as durable and require regular treatment to keep them sound, though they do have a particular elegance. Plastic furniture is inexpensive, durable, light and stackable, ideal as extras.

There is always the option to build some furniture into the fabric of the patio. This is a long term commitment but developing retaining walls into benches, or making use of changes in level to add a bar or side table can be nifty space-saving options. Smart opportunistic adaptations will not only make for a more interesting space it will contribute to an ordered, tailored look. If retaining walls have to be built to produce a level area for paving it is little more work to extend them upward to a convenient height, add a slab of smooth wood and the wall becomes valuable extra seating.

Set into the paving, a fire pit is a dramatic focal point, providing warmth on a chilly evening or a primitive but effective barbecue.

Above left A snug urban courtyard has a stone and timber built-in bench supplemented by ad hoc seating on the wide paved rims of raised beds, leaving just enough room for the table.

Above Pretty in pink, brightly coloured furniture introduces a welcome burst of colour to the patio all year round. Often located outside the main rooms of the house, a patio which looks colourful and attractive through the dull winter months is a real bonus.

ALFRESCO COOKING

For perfect outdoor entertaining a dedicated cooking area, with space for preparation, storage and a space for the barbecue or a built-in barbecue makes the cooks life far easier and ensures they are not stuck in the kitchen while everyone else is outside. To work well there needs to be a fair amount of space allowed in the design for preparation, uncooked food, drinks and all the other paraphernalia that makes life easier when cooking outdoors. A basic stretch of stainless steel, granite or oiled wood would suffice with a brick build barbecue or pizza oven or both. You could include cupboards and a sink, there are even appliances designed for outdoor use.

The alternative is to choose a freestanding barbecue and perhaps a robust outdoor console table for preparation. Even if you choose to use a freestanding barbecue include it in your plans, where will it stand? How much space will it occupy? Where can it be stored? Is it a sufficient distance from flammable materials?

PERGOLAS & SHADE

The term pergola is used to describe a number of different structures, linked arches over paths creating a sheltered walkway as well as a larger, wooden structure used to shade areas set aside for dining and relaxation. The pergola can also be used to clearly define a space for a specific purpose, contribute instant height to a design and provide privacy. The addition of a pergola effectively provides a space with open but apparent walls and a ceiling. How solid these appear will depend on the choice and size of materials from which they are constructed and how heavily they are planted. A metal pergola, left unadorned by plants will be light, airy and serve little practical function, a wooden structure with hefty posts, closely spaced cross beams and a heavy layer of robust vines may be almost impervious to rain as well as sun and prying neighbours.

Deciding on whether and where to include a pergola in your garden at the outset is a must as it throws up many design opportunities which can only be exploited if they are incorporated as the patio is constructed. On a large area of paving it is sensible to cover just part of the area with a pergola, thus you have a choice, sun or no sun depending on the season. The spaces between the supporting posts of the pergola provide large frames to capture the view or focus attention on other garden features. Getting the layout just right, to comfortably accommodate the right sized table and position supports successfully takes thought some thought and is best carried out long before construction starts.

Similarly, if the structure is to be festooned with climbing plants planting pocket need to left around the posts if they are not within reach of the soil at

the edge of the paving. Depending on the plants you choose and how dense you hope the cover will be, it is not essential to allow each post a planting area. These could be in the form of raised beds set around a number of the key posts with walls at about seat height, making occasional seating as well as planting beds.

Most climbing plants once persuaded up the post with stout twine will sprawl across the beams for several meters if left unchecked, though it may be necessary to supplement the beams with some taut lengths of wire to help things along and provide additional support. Evocative of Mediterranean climes, grape vines are a common choice, they are fast growing and will soon provide a verdant ceiling to filter the sun. Late in the summer bunches of grapes should hang below the foliage for eating or wine making, however wasps find the ripening fruit attractive too and can become a pest. Roses, jasmine and honeysuckle are a traditional planting and will provide cascading, colourful scented blooms all summer long. For a robust, jungle covering with blazing autumn colour try *vitis cognetiae*, with its enormous textured green leaves that erupt into a volcano of colour in the autumn. White flowered

Pergolas can span an entire patio; monumental rough columns support a vaulted, verdant roof of metal arcs and vines. The lofty construction dwarfs the table, but the generous height ensures the ceiling does not become oppressive.

An elegantly simple wooden pergola affords some seclusion and defines the eating area in this paved town garden.

Solanum jasminoides has more delicate foliage for a more open canopy whilst *trachelospermum jasminoides* a small leaved evergreen climber with small fragrant flowers is a good choice for year round cover. There are clematis to suit just about any situation and wisteria will provide cascading blue or white racemes of fragrant blooms.

The style and materials of the pergola and its planting should work with the themes of the patio. Rustic poles have a cottage garden or relaxed Mediterranean flavour, smooth planed oak can take on any character depending on how it is shaped, wire work and intricate metal pergolas have a traditions appeal, while scaffolding poles can be used to make something urban and edgy. Depending on the material and the need for planting pockets, the pergola can be built first and the paving floor constructed later around the supports.

Though including a pergola has many advantages, where the paved area is small and the weather variable it may cast shade when sun might be preferred and in some locations it will unreasonably restrict light into the windows it straddles in the winter. There is a vast range of parasols which will do better in this situation, either supported through the table or cantilevered over seating areas on a weighty base. Available in all styles, sizes and colours there is bound to be a parasol to suit your scheme so shop around, often this is a forgotten element of a design yet in the summer months the parasol will dominate the patio and so it should be hardworking and look great.

Parasols are temporary and easily moved to shade just the right spot, canvas canopies are a stylish way of providing shade spanning whichever part of the patio needs protection, they can be removed and stowed away for the winter but many are not easily removed or moved. Many canopies are available with well tested fabrics and a clear UV protection figures and have the added bonus of being rainproof, so meals don't have to be abandoned because of a passing light shower of rain. They can be fixed to poles and tensioned wires or anchored to buildings and are available in interesting three dimensional shapes as well as flat sails.

A light, geometric no-nonsense pergola for a very contemporary garden. A grid of box profile metal elements unadorned by planting provides no shade but will give those enjoying the steamer chairs a feeling of being sheltered.

Planting

It may seem counter-intuitive but plants play a starring role in most patio and courtyard designs. Plants are the props and the ornaments that decorate the patio, they are the scene-setters that help define the style and mood, they are vibrant, verdant and animated breathing life into a scheme, they contribute colour with flowers and foliage and soften the severest of paving. Plants are the ultimate, versatile 'finishing touch'.

As you plan your patio formulating some idea about the planting, where it will be, the style and the type of plants is all part of the process. The detail can come later but raised beds, planting pockets or spaces for plants to cover a pergola all need to go on the plan. If you intend to use good sized pots you need to allow space in your design.

GREEN SCREENS

Plants are not just a tool for getting the aesthetics of the space right they can be of practical use to, generating shade with pergolas festooned with plants has already been discussed but plants can be a great asset in creating privacy without it appearing that the space is oppressively enclosed. A rustling curtain of bamboo, a mass of flowering shrubs or a smartly clipped hedge will all engender a feeling of seclusion when planted around the patio without the stark obviousness of a fence. Some plants may take a while to come into their own but bamboo will quickly form a screen. Some bamboos are rather coarse and prone to brutishness, but the fine leaved, evergreen *phyllostachys nigra* (Black bamboo) or *phyllostachys aurea* are fairly restrained in their habits and unlikely to course a problem, though it is advisable to plant them with a root barrier. This type of screening is best planted in the ground next to the patio, though one way to gain say a couple of feet in height is to plant in a raised bed constructed as part of the scheme.

Lavishly planted raised beds provide a much needed green screen around a roof top terrace.

PLANTS IN POTS

Plants in pots are the simplest and most versatile way to soften the patio and inject vibrant colour with seasonal flowers. As your ideas develop there will probably be certain positions where pots are a must, flanking doorways or a group in a corner or a row of identical pots at the side of the terrace or perhaps a cluster to divide one area from another. Some may be a permanent part of the design, key pieces in setting the mood others may be seasonal planted up to provide an abundance of blooms.

Permanent planted pots should probably be evergreen or at least look good in the coldest months, although you may not use the terrace in the winter you will look out on to it if it is next to the house. Tightly clipped topiary has a formal traditional appeal, though the clean lines of its geometric shapes suit modern minimal designs too. Repetition,

a row of identical plants in identical pots is a simple device used by designers which is easy to replicate successfully and looks particularly impressive when it is done with topiary. Always use an odd number of plants in the row, it always looks better than an even number. Palms are another possibility for this 'backbone' planting, they conjures up a lavish, tropical atmosphere. With their statuesque, architectural forms just a couple of good specimens can do the trick. Small acers, like 'Garnet' and 'Bloodgood' with their delicate, dramatically coloured foliage make fantastic star plants in containers too, though deciduous the silhouette of their framework of branches is beautiful Chose specimens with interesting shapes.

South-facing patios can become real hotspots, so the structural plants need to be real sun lovers, if you want an easy life. Enormous, lobed leaves and the promise of a crop of succulent fruit make the fig

a great choice for clothing a south-facing wall, grey leaved plants and herbs like rosemary, lavender, *cistus* and *artemisia* will also thrive in the heat. While yuccas, phormiums and all succulents should thrive, rather than wilt. Both olive and citrus trees will enjoy a warm spot, olive trees have delicate, pretty greyish foliage and citrus trees offer fragrant blossom and fruit.

Selecting pots for the key permanent plants is as important as the plants themselves, pot and plant should complement each other and the style of the space. You should be able to pass good terracotta on to your grandchildren, not only that but it will look better then than it does today. Good terracotta is beyond fashion and works in many different styles of garden room from traditional to Mediterranean and even contemporary depending on its form. Soft and earthy, the pots are easy to live with and suit a host of planting styles. Some less expensive terracotta can look a little brash, too brick orange. This can be calmed down with wash of very, very dilute lime wash or similarly diluted white emulsion paint. Try a patch first to check you are happy with the effect, the pot sucks in the liquid leaving a dusty bloom. Shinning, angular metal containers tend to fit best in modern gardens, cubes or troughs are practical but

the roots of the plants can get over heated so a lining of polystyrene or thick wodge of newspaper can help.

Stylish wooden Versailles planters have an enduring appeal and a certain formality that suits shaped box and yew as well as citrus plants. As they are wood they will require some maintenance, painting or staining, to guarantee a long life. There are plastic pots, lead containers, reclaimed containers to choose from too, but the important thing in deciding on the pots for key plants is that they work together and enhance your scheme. They do not have to match identically (unless you are trying some repetition) they just need to look as if they belong together and on your patio or courtyard.

Seasonal planting gives enormous scope for enlivening a space with colour. Annuals are the obvious choice, guaranteed to produce a profusion of flowers all summer, though they do need regular feeding with liquid fertilizer to keep the display going. However, there is no reason that flowering herbaceous perennials cannot be potted up to decorate the patio for a season, or perhaps two and then planted out in the garden.

Whatever you grow in pots watering can become a chore. Installing a simple irrigation system can lessen the load. Basic systems available from DIY stores are more than adequate for most patios and court yards. When you are formulating your design look for ways to run the pipes discretely, a tangled web of black irrigation pipes does not look good.

RAISED BEDS

The solution to achieving large blocks of planting where no soil is available, elevating planting areas within the paving or making boundaries between different areas of the garden and adding interest to the paving's structure the raised bed has plenty to offer. With sufficiently wide coping stones, or a timber top they become ad hoc seating, they offer scope to build more generous benches into their structure, offer a raised stage on which sculptures and water features can be shown off and the opportunity to divide and structure space. In some situations, like a completely paved court yard or a roof terrace they are the only way to provide a good amount of soil to house plenty of plants.

The raised beds can be constructed of inexpensive concrete blocks and rendered or faced with the material used for the paving, or the paving can be used to form a coping. Alternatively timber or sleepers can be used to form the walls. The beds will need good drainage either via weep holes, small holes at the base of the walls to allow water to escape. To make maintenance straightforward the beds should be no wider than twice the length of your arm, so you can easily get to weeds colonising the middle of the bed. They can be any shape, straight-sided or curved, whatever the design requires.

Creating a two-tier raised bed introduces more creative planting possibilities.

Neatly lined-up strips of grasses add texture to this minimal garden.

PLANTING IN THE PAVING

Lacing your paving with plants will give a far softer garden floor, though to be successful the plants should be chosen with care and the paving adapted to give the plants the best start possible. It is not just paving in gardens with an informal or cottage garden style that can look good peppered with fragrant herbs, grasses or wild flowers. If the plants are regimented, spiking the paving with a shot of living green in even the most minimal of gardens can be refreshing and uplifting.

Plants can be given a foothold in the paving joints or crammed into spaces made by leaving out a stone or two. Some plants, like the creeping thymes and chamomiles will tolerate being trampled a little and will even give off a burst of herby fragrance when crushed. Thymes will produce a mass of tiny flowers which attract a host of butterflies and bees, something to consider if you favour bare feet in the summer. *Soleirolia* (Mind-your-own-business, Baby's Tears) is a tenacious, if not downright invasive, crisp green, small leaved plants, it will spread and survive where it is hard to believe it can get its roots down. It works well around stepping stones or will sidle along joints in paving but it does come with a warning. However, it is fairly easily removed. *Ajuga reptans* is a less strident alternative, slightly larger but with rich purple foliage, though this plant would prefer not to be trodden upon. Most scree and alpine plants should flourish in compost and grit-filled joints.

In larger planting pockets almost anything which will have enough space to put down its roots can be planted, herbs are successful, while airy, ornamental grasses have a winning way of associating perfectly with natural stone. Floriferous wild flowers, perennials and annuals can all be part of the mix. Plan where to place planting pockets with care, creeping plants like thyme will take a little, light foot traffic but other plants will not and can become a nuisance if there is not enough space to circumnavigate them without colliding with furniture or pots.

The opportunity to add planting to the paved floor can really inspire but it adds another element to maintain. One of the benefits of a paved garden floor is its immutable good looks – a flick of the broom is for the most part all that is required to keep it spick and span. Plants, unfortunately, are not that reliable and if the plants look drab, unkempt and lacklustre so will the terrace.

Water

Water is a powerful decorative element that can be harnessed to enliven any patio. Imaginative use of moving water in a patio can bring movement, sound and sparkle to the space. For a dash of serenity a still pool will mirror the sky and offer the opportunity to soften the paving with a smattering of aquatic plants. A traditional fountain, water wall or bubbling feature will cool the air – the more the water jumps, gushes and cascades the greater the spectacle.

There is an amazing array of ways in which water can be wrought into a design, from slim trickling rills in the paving and raised reflective pools to exciting jets of water crashing onto boulders and shimmering metallic or glass walls glossed with a flowing sheet of moving water. The final choice will depend on the space available and the effect needed. Vertical and wall mounted features are well suited to small spaces as are canals running under metal grids which do not interrupt the continuity of the paved floor. In more lavish schemes larger features can be designed. Vertical and freestanding features can make strong focal points, guiding the eye around the patio. After dark, carefully illuminating moving water produces a visual feast of twinkling light.

Beyond its aesthetic role and the ability to inject a touch of pizzazz into an outdoor space, water can be of practical use in masking background noise, replacing the low rumble of traffic and chat of neighbours. Depending on the level of noise to be disguised water can produce anything from a gentle plash to a crashing torrent. It is unlikely to solve a problem completely but having a soothing source of sound nearby reduces the impact of the sound beyond.

Most water features will require the installation of a reservoir, pump, a series of pipes and electricity, this all needs to be planned at the design stage so it can be neatly and efficiently constructed as the patio is built. Electrical installation should be carried out by a suitably qualified individual and in line with all regulations. 'Stand alone' water features are a carry in, quick fix only needing an electrical connection and to be filled with water to begin. These offer the flexibility to move the feature or change it when fashions shifts or you tire of it.

If you are designing your own canal or bubble feature always buy a pump with an adjustable flow. Getting the flow of water just right can be a matter of trial and error, adjusting the flow will allow the water to be transformed from a gentle trickle to a gushing stream. The amount of water splashing from features with falling water can be a difficulty if the flow is not just right. There is also a matter of tuning the sound, so it is musical and pretty rather than clumsy and crashing.

Clockwise from top left A rill and the strip of water trickling its length need not be lavish to have impact. Raised from the floor and set atop a stout wall around an area of paving this small rustic rill lined with terracotta half pipes gains impact from being elevated to where it can be better appreciated; Slipping from a flat metal shoot this free falling slice of water vanishes through a strong metal grille producing a good amount of splashing; Monumental in its construction, dominating the rendered and painted end wall of an enclosed gravel patio this colossal feature provides plenty of sound and drama to enliven the space; A simple rectangular pool adds a concentrated hit of pattern and colour to this paving with its punchy mosaic.

WATER SAFETY

Children can drown in very shallow standing water, so in gardens where children play choose bubbling features or water walls which have no open water.

Lighting

To continue enjoying life outdoors as twilight falls on barmy summer evenings and bring a touch of magic to your patio, you will need to plan some lighting in your design.

Clever but not necessarily costly, lighting can transform a straightforward space by day into something quite enchanting by night. Often the best schemes for creating a magical mood are subtle, restrained with fittings which are invisible by day. Though there are an immense number of lumieres on the market small spotlights on swivel fittings are versatile, easy to install and can be used to create staggering effects.

Lighting can be divided into three categories, practical lighting, including flood lights and security lights, lighting for atmosphere and temporary lighting, provided by candles, lanterns and party lights. Practical lighting may already be in place but if not, while the patio construction and wiring is underway it may be a good time to consider including some. These lights are often on motion sensors to provide a deterrent to intruders and a good level of light for making your way around the outside of the house at night. This type of practical lighting should be on a different circuit to the mood lighting so it can be switched off when required.

Atmospheric lighting, shining through planting, washing paved and vertical surfaces and illuminating focal points is valuable even when it is too cold to use the patio, giving tantalizing view of the garden from the house after dark. Small, discreet spotlights on swivel mountings can be used to dramatic effect, to up light objects when placed at ground level, to light objects from above when fixed on a wall or pergola or cut objects with a beam of light throwing its texture or contours into sharp relief. The beam of light from a spot is narrow, but its exact width (given as an angle) will determine the effect achieved. If the posts of a pergola or a slight sculpture are to be lit a narrow beam will be required, washing a surface with triangles of light might require a wider beam.

Lights set into the paving flush with the surface are neat, arranged in strips or sweeping arcs they can be used to delineate the shapes of the paving in the darkness leading the eye into the garden. They are a good method of illuminating lights to ensure they are clearly visible. These must be installed as part of the construction process and the wiring accommodated below the paving. Cutting the apertures may be beyond the amateur and all electrical installation should be carried out by a suitably qualified individual in accordance with local regulations.

A way of avoiding all this fuss is to use solar lights. Though they may not match the intensity of light from standard lighting, they are immensely flexible and child's play to install. Many units require no wiring, each having its own tiny panel to collect the energy from the sun's rays and store them until later. In other systems a number of lights are wired together to a larger panel which can be placed in a discrete location. Most come equipped with a sensor which illuminates them at dusk and turns them off at dawn. The obvious drawback is that should the weather be dull for a number of days the lights will fail to recharge. These lights can be dropped into place any time.

Capturing the view

The view across the pool affords an uninterrupted view of the sea and land beyond. The stone columns at the side of the view frame a manageable snap shot.

When positioning the patio the view, if there is one to be had, will have been a major factor. Often, however, small patios dedicated to dining are, by their nature, inward looking spaces.

Diners sit facing each other across the table, glimpsing what lies beyond. On larger patios with space for less formal seating having a fantastic landscape or cityscape to enjoy can be a great bonus. Where the view is irresistible the table can be orientated to give the best views of the garden or panorama beyond.

Capturing the view is not merely about placing the patio where the view can be enjoyed, it is about managing the outlook to get the most from what is on offer. Often providing a point of interest in the foreground will help make the view more impressive, giving it more context. Framing certain highlights whatever they may be, perhaps an historic building, a clump of trees on a hillside or a dramatic range of industrial chimneys, with planting, trees or the supports of the pergola will make the scene more digestible. Avoid using strong features which will detract from the inherent beauty of the location, gilding the lily.

A metal pergola focuses activity on a large terrace in just the right spot to enjoy the magical view.

SCREENS & BOUNDARIES

Patios are places to relax and be sociable, comfortable places that suggest an escape or freedom from the duties and responsibilities of everyday life. For most people for that liberation to be successful the space needs to feel private with a degree of seclusion. Pergolas and sail canopies provide a partial patio roof if there is a need to restrict the view from above. Screening and setting the boundaries are slightly different, screening is to create privacy while the boundaries of the patio are also part of framing it and establishing its place in the garden.

In windy locations a screen can also provide shelter from the prevailing wind, creating a protected nook. Fencing, stone walls, trellis, a severely clipped hedge or a luxuriant bank of leafy planting will all do the job, selecting the right one is a matter of sticking with your style ideas and your budget. Stone walls involve a significant investment, whereas a couple of panels of off-the-shelf trellis is a comparatively low cost, quick fix. Solid screens will provide the most privacy, trellis once festooned with climbers will obscure the view. If protection from the wind is a prime concern then a slightly open screen or 'hit-and-miss' fence may be a more practical solution as wind tends to tumble over solid structure, working into turbulent eddies on the other side. More open structures allow the wind through but lessen its force. In general a screen will protect an area equivalent to twice its height from the wind, remember for the most part people using the patio will be seated.

Defining the boundary of the patio and providing it with a frame is part of melding this outdoor room into the fabric of the garden. A patio raised above the level of the garden will need a wall or barrier to prevent people toppling into the garden below, but otherwise barriers can be visual rather than practical. A sprawl of planting arranged around the borders of the patio, with gaps left to allow passage from one area to another, may be all that's required to link the patio to the garden. A clipped hedge, like box, makes a more formal barrier, though a tidy row of lavender for example, will have a similar but softer effect. Including a low fence or wall may give the patio a greater feeling of permanence and importance. Low walls with generous, wide smooth coping stones, tiles or planed wood make valuable extra seating. Or alternatively, a double low stone wall with space for soil and plants could be used. In choosing materials, go back to the idea of the limited palette of materials to achieve a calculated, designed look.

Opposite top Though very open, this decorative, geometric timber screen provides a feeling of seclusion and separation, providing an interesting back drop for the terrace which changes as the sun moves and shadow shift.

Opposite far right A woven willow fence is a fitting screen for a relaxed and natural scheme.

A mild steel screen creates privacy when seated, but a slot allows a view beyond when standing.

Paths

There is normally a definite hierarchy of paths in any garden design: the first might be called practical or primary paths. This does not mean they should not be beautiful but rather that these are the main arteries of the garden, affording passage from street to house, house to garage and other significant areas.

These paths should be wide, ideally allowing two people to walk side by side and easy to walk or wheel things along. In most cases these will be the most formal, sensible paths in the garden. These paths should be between 1 and 1.2 m (3 and 4 ft) wide. The second are the less important paths in the garden, linking various garden rooms or points of interest or just a designer's trick to highlight a particular view or focal point. These do not need to be so wide, the practicality of the surface is a matter of choice dependent upon whether you want to children to be able to use wheeled toys, wheelbarrows to be pushed easily or to slow progress and add texture with an uneven surface. These paths might be as little as 61 cm (24 in) wide.

The third category of paths are the least formal, they may in fact be stepping stones rather than a full blown path. These routes might be to less frequented areas of the garden, or provide adventurous routes through areas of planting. These paths may be very narrow, just 30 cm (12 in) wide, and so uneven as to require a slow pace and some fancy foot work. There is plenty of room for wit, experimentation and fun when planning these routes.

PLANNING A ROUTE

One of the basic rules for adding paths to a garden is that they must lead somewhere; there must be a destination, even if it is as clearly contrived as a bench or sculpture. The shortest route from A to B is not necessarily the best course for a path. In formal gardens long poker straight paths may fit the bill but gently curving paths can be used to carve out new areas in the garden, outlining beds for planting. Paths can be made to meander so different parts of the garden are revealed at every turn. Too many small changes of direction, resulting in an intricately fashioned, wiggling path can make matters frustrating and result in unofficial short-cuts being forged through planting by regular garden users. Drawing curved paths on plans can be misleading, once translated to the ground the curve will become more compact, less sweeping as your view point changes.

Clockwise from top left A path with real character, meandering slightly, this marvellously relaxed track of rounded pebbles is a breeze to walk on but is obviously of no serious intent; Composed of stone flags which sit cordially against the stone of the house, this purposeful path leads straight to the front door; With just enough of a curve to keep one wondering what is around the corner, the random stone surface suits informal, indirect paths; The sculpture provides the destination and focal point for this stretch of path which then continues beyond the artwork.

HOW WIDE?

As well as having a bearing on its practicality, the width of a path will also have an impact on how quickly it is navigated. Narrow paths encourage haste; if the surrounding planting is high they can engender a feeling of disquiet and claustrophobia. If a path is bounded, even if it is only on one side, by a tall hedge, wall or imposing planting a generous path will feel more comfortable. To engender a relaxed atmosphere, paths should be wide and open. If a route passes through an area of planting, the illusion of a wide thoroughfare can be arranged even if the paved area of the path is not as wide as it might be by using turf or ground hugging planting like thyme or chamomile at each side. Through woodland a similar effect can be achieved by opening up the area along the sides of the path. A path that is 106.5–122 cm (42–48 in) wide will allow two people to stroll side by side; 61–91.5 cm (24–36 in) is a comfortable width for one person, while a 30 cm (12 in) wide path will encourage a more hurried pace.

Paths and planting drawn on a plan respect each other's boundaries, in real, flourishing gardens however burgeoning beds are likely to spill flowers and foliage onto paths, so in planning routes through planting allow for this seasonal abundance, or if you are a lover of neat edges plant less fulsome plants alongside the path.

The ample width of this flag path is perfectly balanced with the abundant tall planting it is edged with on both sides. Plants loll onto the paving and there is still plenty of room to pass.

MATERIALS

There is arguably an even wider range of materials to choose from when designing a path than there is for a terrace as, for less frequently trodden paths at least, there is not the same need for a level, hardwearing surface. Main paths must be durable and afford easy passage in all weathers but in other areas there is room for some less conventional and less convenient surfaces. Crushed shells, log rounds, glass mulch, wood chip, loose slate, wood setts, reclaimed sleepers, ceramic tiles and cocoa shells might all be used.

A path should be in harmony with its surroundings, reflecting and enhancing the mood of the spaces through which it passes, the materials from which it is constructed impart a huge part of its character. In small gardens choosing a collection of two or three types of paving materials, a brick, gravel and a flag for example, and using them in different combinations around the garden gives the garden a designed, coherent look. In larger gardens with distinctive

garden rooms paths can be tailored to suit the style of the area they serve. Light, bright coloured paths will demand more attention than those made of darker materials like brick.

Frequently trodden paths need a surface which will wear well, does not become slippery when wet and is easily traversed without thought for where each foot is placed. These paths must be practical but they should also be beautiful and a pleasure to use, they are after all the threads which hold the garden together. Secondary paths may be made up of less practical materials, while informal paths can be slightly challenging to negotiate. It is important to match the surface of the path to its use, a simple, narrow gravel path to the compost heaps may seem adequate but a smooth paved path is far easier to negotiated with a heavy wheel barrow and simpler to keep clean. A cobbled path to the front door may have the cottage garden look you are hoping for but the uneven surface is not easy to walk upon. In large gardens there may be a call for a network of service paths at the back of deep beds. These routes are purely practical and inexpensive materials will suffice.

PATTERN

The materials you chose and the route it takes will both contribute to the character of the finished path but the pattern you decorate the surface of the path with is the final factor in determining how it works. Even once the choice of materials has been made the way they are arranged will have a huge impact on whether they lead the eye quickly along its length to a focal point or vista or slow the pace. A pattern can be directional or static, while some are strongly directional others may be less so.

The easiest example to demonstrate this effect is brick paving: laying the bricks in a running bond along the length of the path produces a strongly directional pattern, pulling the eye and the walker quickly along the path. The path will appear longer and narrower than if the bricks were arranged across the path. Brick laid in a stretcher bond across the path slows progress and appears to widen the path as the direction of the pattern runs across the path. Brick arranged in a basket weave produces a static pattern with no direction. The orientation of any material can be orchestrated to the same effect. Armed with this knowledge paths can be lengthened, views and features highlighted and space manipulated to suit your ends.

Functioning like an enormous arrow pointing the way, the brick laid in a running bond inextricably focuses attention on the sculpture and the arch beyond.

Rectangular stones arranged along the length of this narrow route give the illusion of lengthening this hurried path.

Stepping stones

In just a few hours a new route across the garden can be forged with stepping stones.

Stepping stones can be an expedient design solution to guiding people around the garden without the expense and upheaval of constructing a path, however the partial nature of the path can have other design advantages too. A carefully placed run of stepping stones can subtly lead the eye to a particular point in the distance, punctuating an expanse of gravel or lawn without the dominant solidity of a path which may overcomplicate a space. Stepping stones are, needless to say, practical too, level stones placed to match a comfortable walking pace make an all weather route across lawns or through planting. The stones can be eye-catching and decorative, enlivening the garden floor with a burst of colour or an inconspicuous colour, set low in the turf so as to be almost invisible.

The 'stones' themselves might be stone but they could be mosaic, wood, natural rocks, concrete, brick, painted concrete or pebble mosaic depending on what suits the situation best. As they are a small scale project requiring little financial outlay and wreak no great harm on the garden, they offer an opportunity to express yourself and test your creative edge.

Practical stones should be set a comfortable stride apart; this is easily tested by laying the stones on the ground along the proposed route. To encourage slower progress stones can be arranged in a broken pattern, so no rhythm can be established, where each step has to be considered.

Clockwise from top left Set low in the turf so mowing is an easy matter, square stones make a practical route across the lawn; Closely spaced pieces of timber make a striped path of timber and grass, which is practical and simple to negotiate at speed. Set in the ground, hard wood or treated soft wood will give several years' good service before rotting; These smooth hunks of granite set in a moss make a most impressive, stepping-stone path, with a Japanese flavour. Though safe and smooth, each step would require some concentration; Large smooth stones make a very purposeful, narrow path through low planting. The contrast between the dark stones and the paler gravel make for a bold design.

Pools

Not just essential for the convenience of the bathers, a good area of paving around a pool is essential to anchor it to the garden if this rather alien feature is to be successfully and seamlessly linked to the surrounding area.

The style of the pool itself and the surrounding garden will dictate the style of paving most suited to the job, a slick contemporary pool will benefit from equally slick, stylish paving but there is an increasing tendency for more naturally shaped pools which demand a more organic approach to the paving. Large flat rocks being incorporated around the pools edge as well as naturalistic planting.

Bathers emerging from the water will be far less prone to slip on textured paving, but the material chosen still needs to be comfortable for bare feet. In general the considerations are much the same as designing a patio or terrace. There should be enough space for all the activities likely to be conducted on the poolside, enjoying the sun, dining, barbecuing and perhaps an area of shade. For safety and maintenance easy access is needed all around the pool, unless of course it is an infinity pool. There is an understandable impulse to frame the pool with a neat rectangle of paving, equal on all sides, but this may not be the best use of resources. Consider the path of the sun and the views and determine where the main seating areas should be and tailor the shape accordingly. Secure barriers should be installed as part of the landscaping around any pool, especially where children, animals or the elderly may tumble into the pool.

The area around the pool is as important as the pool. In most climates a pool cannot be used all year round but a well-landscaped surround, with good paving, furniture, planting and lighting will make the pool area an appealing place to be whatever the weather.

CONSTRUCTION BASICS

Setting out

The basic principles for laying paving are very similar whatever surface material you are planning to use. This section goes through each part of the construction process, step by step. The process is not hard to master but does require a fair amount of physical work. If you are a complete novice it might make sense to cut your teeth on a small project, honing your skills and testing your endurance, before launching into a very large patio project.

Most pros will use a laser level to set out or mark out the extent of the paving on the ground but the job can easily be done with two long tape measures, a spirit level and a string line. Setting out is an important process and requires some care but it is not difficult. Not only are the boundaries of your design transferred to the ground once it is finished it is a good time to step back and consider- are the proportions right? Is it cutting across or obstructing any important features? Is it big enough? Does it just need shifting a few meters to the right/ left? All of these problems are easily solved at this stage.

Before you begin the site should be fairly clear, areas of tall vegetation cut down, so pegs and string lines can run across the site easily. Building over old foundations has an obvious appeal, saving time and materials but it is seldom successful. If the old surface failed it was quite possibly caused by unstable foundations. If you are investing in new stones and your efforts in developing the perfect design then it is best to clear the old paving and begin again. That is not to say you cannot reuse some of the materials or even sell the old paving stones.

Available from most DIY stores, marking out spray is an effective way to mark out shapes and is easily scuffed away if you make a mistake.

MARKING OUT A CIRCLE

If you have a good scale plan you can fix the centre point of the circle in the garden by a process known as triangulation, this means you chose the two most practical fixed points on a plan and measure how far the centre of the circle is from each. Scale up the measurements so you can transfer them to the ground. Then using two long tape measures, measure from the same fixed points in the garden using the scaled up measurements. Where the two tapes cross is the centre of your circle. This will give an accurate representation of what is on your plan, however, if this is a freestanding circle of paving and nothing else depends on its accurate location and nothing is to be built near it you could just judge it by eye. Either way when you are happy with the location of the centre of the circle bang in a peg, something the end of the tape can be hooked over. Attach the tape to the post, then extend the tape to the radius of the circle

and pulling it taut walk around the peg marking the circumference of the circle with sand or a marking out spray.

MARKING OUT A RECTANGLE

If the area to be paved is against the house this can form the base line for marking out, otherwise you will need to establish a base line, one side of the rectangle by a process of triangulation (see page 84), find the position of the two corners, knock in a peg and fasten a string line between them. Next, mark out the sides by extending the string line at 90° to the base line the correct distance and knocking in a peg. There are two ways to check the corner is 90°, the first is by using a builder's square, a large triangular tool placed in the corner to verify the position of the strings is accurate (if you do not

Using a builder's square is a simple way to ensure corners are exactly 90°.

want to purchase one of these they are easily made with three pieces of straight timber, it does not need to be a work of art the but there must be a good 90° angle at the corner). The second is based on Pythagoras' Theorem, a triangle with sides in the ratio 3:4:5 will always have a right angle opposite the hypotenuse (the long side). Put simply, measure along one string 30 cm (12 in) from the corner and make a mark, measure 40 cm (16 in) along the other and make a mark, measure the distance between the marks across the corner, if it is 50 cm (20 in) you have a right angle at the corner. Once you have the two sides, join the pegs with the string line to make the final side. One final way to check you have the perfect rectangle rather than one that leans slightly is to measure both diagonals, they should be the same.

MARKING OUT CURVES

A sweeping curved edge to a patio or a meandering path is slightly more time consuming to set out, but once a good base line is in place it is fairly simple. Having said all this if you are merely adding a path to a garden with an existing floor plan I think it is far better done by eye. In this situation mark it out with marking out spray, sand, ropes or a hose initially and walk along it, see how it fits with the rest of the garden. The edges can be moved or scrubbed out until it is just right, then marked permanently with sand or spray marker. If the path is part of a larger scheme it is probably best to work from the plan to ensure it ends up just where it is supposed to!

Start by selecting a base line on your plan, it may be there is a readymade baseline in the form of fence if not draw one on the plan. Next measure offsets, lines at 90° to the base line, at regular intervals from the base line to the edge of the path. Now transfer the base line from the plan to the garden using the same method as establishing a base line for rectangles above. If using an existing feature as a baseline you can skip this step. Now fix points along the curve by transferring the offsets from the scale plan to the ground. You will need two tapes, one stretched along the baseline and one to measure the offsets and a builder's triangle to check your offsets come off the base line at 90°. The frequency of the off sets depends on the intricacy of the curve. Once each point has been marked it should be simple to join the points using marking spray or sand to replicate the curve on the plan.

In this small area where the path is to be bounded by drifts of planting, laying the path out with a hose or rope by eye is an adequate solution.

Getting the fall right

Paved surfaces should have a slight, often imperceptible slope known as 'the fall' built into them. This ensures that rainwater drains efficiently from the surface of the paving rather than collecting in puddles.

If the paving adjoins the house the fall should run away from the house, some large areas of paving will have a fall running in two directions to ensure water can drain away quickly. The exact fall required will depend on the surface material you are using, the greatest fall is needed on the paving with the most uneven surface, very riven stone as water will find it hardest to drain from these surfaces, whereas polished granite or limestone will allow water to slip away easily.

For small areas of paving it is enough for the water to drain into an area of planting or lawn, so long as this soil does not already have a drainage problem. In confined areas, like a walled court yard or where water is collecting over a larger area drains will need to be installed to channel the water into a soak away or the drainage system. The drain might take the form of a perforated pipe buried in a gravel-filled gulley, an open brick or sett drainage channel, a precast concrete channel or a precast channel with a metal grill lid. The perforated pipe in a gravel channel is the simplest to construct and can be easily worked into a design, open brick and sett channels can be decorative and used to create interest in the paved surface, cast concrete channels are a more utilitarian solution, though they may sit well in a stripped back, urban design.

The fall is normally expressed as a ratio, 1:60 for example. This means that for every 60 cm (24 in) you travel across the paving it should fall by 1 cm (or rise by 1 cm if you are travelling in the opposite direction.) It can be worked out in any unit so longs as both units are the same. So to give a 1:60 fall, a terrace 6 m (20 ft) wide will be 10 cm (4 in) higher at one side than the other.

MINIMUM FALLS

Block/brick paving	1:60
Smooth flagstones	1:60
Rough, uneven or riven flagstones	1:50
Setts and cobbles	1.50
Pebble mosaic	1:40

Paths can be built with a camber to ensure good drainage.

TRANSFERRING THE FALL TO THE GROUND

At this point the extent of the paving is marked out on the ground and excavation is yet to begin, you know what fall you need for the paving to shed water efficiently. What you need to know is where the finished level of your paving will fall across the site so you can excavate to the correct depth. There are plenty of ways to do this, once again a pro would use a laser level which is quick and accurate but for most small domestic projects the method described below is good enough.

The first thing to get straight is that any paving by the house should sit at least 15 cm (6 in) below the DPC (damp proof course). Having taken this into consideration decide just where you want surface of the highest end of your patio to sit, away from the house it may be at the existing level of the lawn. Knock a peg in just to the side of the marked out area at the high end so a good portion is left above ground (this is referred to as a datum peg). All levels on the site will be relative to this point. Measure down from the top of this peg to the proposed finished level. Add the amount of fall you need across the whole patio (calculated from the figures on page 85) to the measurement you have just taken. This tells you how much lower the low end of the finished level of the patio needs to be than the top of the datum peg. Knock in a peg with its top level with the datum peg at the far end of the area, use a spirit level and a long straight piece of wood to ensure they are level. You may need to knock in a couple of intermediate posts to transfer the level. It is now easy to judge how deep to excavate by referring to the pegs. (This may sound difficult but it is far simpler when you actually do it.)

The string stretched at finished level across the site ensures paving is laid to achieve the correct fall.

Once the area is excavated, use the datum peg to set up a series of pegs at finished paving height across the site. Draw a string fixed at finished paving level from the datum peg across the excavated area to the peg at the low end of the site, begin by getting the string level, this is easiest to do with a spirit level which hangs on the string. Once the string is level between the two pegs, lower it on the peg at the low end of the site by the total fall required across the paving. This string line now represents the finished surface level across the paving. Drive in as many pegs as you feel you may need to refer to. On a small site it may be sufficient to set up strings at 90° at finished level height along two sides of the excavated area, whereas a large area may need a grid of pegs.

Good foundations

The unseen, unglamorous construction work that goes on to support any sensational paved surface will partly determine just how long it goes on looking sensational. Rigid paved surfaces need a sound rigid foundation, any movement in the foundation will crack the paved surface allowing in water and frost which will further damage the surface.

The exact requirement for foundations is dictated by the material, the level of traffic and the type of ground you are building on. For this reason it is difficult to give hard and fast rules and the information here should be modified to match local conditions. If you are carrying out the work yourself and are unsure of the depth of foundations required for your project it is worth consulting a local builder.

Site preparation requires the excavation of all the top soil containing organic material. The actual depth required will depend on local conditions. Unstable ground or soft spots will need more material removed. The fall needed in the final surface should be reflected in the depth of the area excavated. If you want the paving to sit at ground level then obviously the depth of soil removed should be at least equal to the depth of the sub-base required, plus the thickness of the paving material with the correct depth added to allow for the bedding material.

The foundation or sub-base for most paving will consist of a layer of compacted hardcore or scalping, the thickness of the material will depend on the paving chosen. This is best compacted with a vibrating plate (these are readily available for hire, though a roller could be used. The paving is laid on this foundation or sub-base with a bedding, depending on the style of paving this might be a 1: 3 mortar or sand for bricks, paviours or for lightly used paving where plants are being used to fill mortar joints. The chart below gives an indication of the foundation or sub-base required for each type of paving in most garden situation where there is just pedestrian traffic. Specialist suppliers should be able to supply specifications for the exact depth of sub-base recommended for their product.

A vibrating plate is the easiest way to compact a sub-base of scalping.

MATERIAL	SUB-BASE	BEDDING	JOINTS/POINTS
Concrete and stone flags	7.5–10 cm (3–4 in) compacted hardcore or scalping	3.5 cm (1¼ in) 1:4 cement and grit sand mortar or 2.5–3.5 cm (1–1¼ in) grit sand	1:3 mortar or for narrow joints 1:3 dry mix soft sand and cement watered in or butt jointed or loose gravel
Bricks and engineering bricks (approx. 6.5 cm/2½ in thick)	15 cm (6 in) compacted hardcore or scalping	5 cm (2 in) grit sand bed (usual) or 3.5 cm (1¼ in) 1:4 cement and grit sand mortar for areas of heavy very use	Butt jointed with kiln dried sand or 1:4 dry mix soft sand and cement brushed into cracks
Brick paviours (approx. 3.5 cm/1¼ in thick)	10 cm (4 in) compacted hardcore or scalping	4 cm (1½ in) 1:5 cement to grit sand base	1:3 cement and soft sand mortar
Paving blocks/block paviours (approx. 6 cm/ 2½ in thick)	8–10 cm (3¼–4 in) compacted hardcore or scalping	6 cm (2½ in) grit sand	Butt jointed, vibrated into position once laid and kiln dried sand vibrated into joints
Granite and other setts	15 cm (6 in) compacted hardcore or scalping	5 cm (2 in) grit sand or 4:1 dry mix sand and cement	3:1 mortar or poured pitch (bitumen a traditional method)
Gravel	10 cm (4 in) compacted hardcore. In areas of very light use gravel can be spread on weed suppressing membrane laid on top soil stripped of vegetation		
Bark/wood chips	10 cm (4 in) compacted hardcore or as gravel above		

If the surface vegetation is cut back the ground can be covered with a good-quality weed-suppressing membrane pinned down securely, with a good overlap where pieces meet gravel can be spread on the surface. Though not suited to vehicular traffic this method is fine for seating areas and some paths and allows the surface to be peppered with plants, popped though holes in the membrane. The same applies for wood chip.

Laying flags

Flags can be laid in one of two ways, either on a full bed of mortar also referred to as a mortar bed or by what is known as the five spot method or spot bedding.

Using five heaps of mortar which squash easily to accommodate the unevenness in the stone is easy to master but not as effective as a full bed of mortar.

THE FIVE SPOT METHOD

The five spot method involves bedding the slab onto generous spots of mortar one at each corner and one in the middle, the flag is then rested on top of the spots and tapped down, with a rubber mallet, to the correct level. The five spot method is often easier for novices as getting the flags level, even if they vary a great deal in thickness, by flattening the five heaps of mortar under the flag is fairly easy. There are several problems with using this method, however, even though the spots of mortar spread out as the flag is tapped into place spaces will be left under the paving and the flag is not fully supported. This means the flag may break, water can collect under the paving causing settling or damage from the process of freezing and thawing. Pointing is also made more difficult as the mortar slips under the flag. So though this may appear a simple option it is far better to master using a full bed of mortar.

MORTAR BED METHOD

This method requires a bed of mortar about 5 cm (2 in) deep (this will compact to give about 3.5 cm/1¼ in when the flag is tapped down) to be spread where the flag is to be placed. Once the mortar is spread use a trowel to create furrows in the surface to allow the mortar to move as the flag is tapped level. The difficulty comes when flags are very uneven, they may have a lump in the middle or they may be an inch or so thicker at one end than the other. In this situation the mortar bed has to be adjusted to fit, something which becomes easier with practice. If you don't get it just right first time the flag can be lifted and mortar added or taken away. Using this method the whole flag is evenly supported and there should be no voids under the paving to cause problems.

1

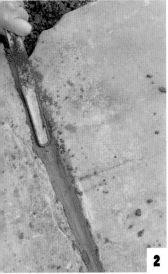

2

3

Joints & pointing – filling the gaps

The final stage in creating paving pointing can be the triumphant finishing touch which pulls the surface together or lets it down. The most glorious stone or tiles can be marred by bad pointing. The function is not just aesthetic, it makes the paved floor one continuous surface, impervious to rain and frost damage.

Step 1 Take a lump of mortar on a large trowel and use a smaller trowel to feed the mortar into the joints. Pack the mortar in with the side of the small trowel.

Step 2 Once the joint is packed full of mortar, smooth it down using a pointing iron.

Some surfaces are arranged with alternative filling between the paving stones, small pebbles or plants such as thyme or camomile might be used. Materials like brick or granite setts and paviours can be butted close together with no joint visible.

MORTAR JOINTS

Pointing should be carried out soon after the paving has been laid, though it is important to wait for the right weather conditions, rain makes the task impossible, frosts that evening will weaken the mortar, and if the weather is very hot the mortar can dry out before it has a chance to cure properly, resulting in a weak joint. Only mix a small amount of mortar at any time, as you will use it up slowly and it dries out quickly. The best way to get the mortar into the joints is by using two trowels, a large brick trowel and a small round-ended trowel or pointing trowel. Take a lump of mortar on the large trowel and use the smaller trowel to feed the mortar into the joints. Pack the mortar in with the side of the small trowel. There is a risk the pointing will stain the surface of the stones, particularly if the stone is very pale and porous so it is important to be as precise as possible when filling the joints.

Once the joint is packed full of mortar it is finished with a pointing iron, though a length of copper pipe or garden hose will do the job just as well. It is dragged across the surface of the mortar to give a neat finish which also makes the mortar more resistant to frost and rain. Try not to end up with joints which are deep grooves as these are likely to collect detritus and make the area hard to sweep clean. When the pointing begins to harden, sweep across, not along the joints to clean the surface.

MIXING MORTAR

Mortar is a mixture of builder's sand, cement and water. Adding a plasticizer makes the mortar easier to use, a squirt of washing up liquid will do the trick. Colours and hardeners can also be added to the mix if required.

The mix: for heavily used areas mix three parts sand to one part cement, for lighter traffic four to one will suffice. The quantities need to be reasonably accurate but are generally measured by the shovel load, three shovels of sand to one of cement for three to one mortar. The mortar needs to be a fairly dry mix, holding together but crumbly.

Always wear gloves and take great care when using cement as it is corrosive and will burn skin and eyes. Keep skin covered and wear safety goggles if needed.

HOW TO MAKE MORTAR

1. Put the soft sand and cement into a wheel barrow or large tub and mix until they are a consistent colour. Or use a cement mixer.
2. Make a well in the centre and add water and the plasticizer. Add a little at first and mix.
3. If more water is required add more and mix thoroughly until the mortar is of a consistent consistency throughout.

SLURRY POINTING

For paving where there is a high number of joints relative to the area pointing by hand becomes incredibly time consuming, especially on a fair-sized area. In these situation slurry pointing can be used, a very wet mortar mix is poured over the surface and pushed around with a broom to fill the joints. The excess is swept away and the surface washed or swept clean. This method is quick and works well for setts and cobbles. However, it is very messy and will probably leave a haze on the surface of the stones. This will eventually wear away on most stones but it may stain pale, porous materials. Very uneven stones with deep dips and cracks can also cause a problem as the slurry gets trapped.

THE MORTAR GUN

At the other end of the spectrum from the slurry pointing is the very accurate gun pointing. It produces fantastic joints, with a neat finish and good mortar mixed to suit the equipment used. The process is a little like icing a cake, the gun forces the mortar though a perfectly sized nozzle into the joint – clean and reasonably quick.

RESIN OR POLYMERIC JOINTING MEDIUM

For those new to paving these fantastic products are a real blessing. No need to worry about the intricacies of mixing mortar, no careful packing of mortar into joints and no worries about staining. Just brush the dry powder into the joints, finish the joints and wait. The compound sets on its own to produce a durable, shrink-proof, weed-resistant joint. There are just two draw backs: you have to work reasonably quickly as the product hardens when it comes into contact with the air (it comes in sealed containers and as soon as it is opened the clock is ticking), and the second is cost as it is significantly more expensive than mortar but not prohibitively so for the benefits gained.

If the joints in large stone flags are colonised by plants it still leaves plenty of space to tread without crushing the plants, though plants like thyme and camomile will survive a little light foot traffic.

BUTT JOINTING

Where paving units are placed against each other as is commonly the case with bricks or concrete paviours kiln dried sand is brushed into the joints to lock the surface together. After a month or two it may be necessary to top up the joints as the sand settles a little.

PLANTED JOINTS

Including plants in a paved garden floor injects it with life and colour. To make space for plants in a paved surface either planting pockets can be left in the paving or some joints left without mortar. Plug plants can be crammed into the joints and the joint filled with a layer of gritty compost, topped with gravel or grit. Planting pockets can be treated in the same way, though you could start with larger plants in say 9 cm (3 in) pots. The key to success is choosing the right plants. Some plants, often described as mat forming, will spread out across the paving, creating soft patches of green often studded with blooms. In less structured paving where larger plants can be shown there are plenty of species to select from, depending on the mood of the space.

Laying bricks, block paviours & setts

Bricks, paviours and setts can be laid in a number of different ways. Most commonly they are laid on a bed of grit sand to create a flexible surface, or on a mortar or dry mortar mix bed like flags.

Bricks and some setts have even straight sides, this means they can be laid butt jointed, in other words one paving unit is placed right up against the next. This does not mean the process can be slapdash, the bricks or sets have to be placed carefully, pushed together as tightly as possible so the joint pattern looks right. Set on a sand bed the paving will need a good retaining edge to hold the floor together. This is normally the same or contrasting brick for brick surfaces but could be a decorative or utilitarian concrete kerb. The edging is set on the same foundation as the paving but is bedded in concrete with about 10 cm (4 in) of haunching on the garden side of the kerb. Haunching is mortar built up against the kerb to hold it is place, the top is normally sloped.

Laying bricks or paviours butt jointed on sand is one of the easiest methods for first timers to achieve a good finish with little fuss. There is very little mortar or concrete to deal with and no pointing. Setts can be a little more difficult to lay as they can vary greatly in depth and some individual bedding will be necessary.

Laying brick or setts on a mortar bed to produce a rigid surface is much the same but a mortar bed is used and the joints can be left open if required. Pointing the joints of any fair-sized piece of brick or sett paving is a daunting undertaking, the joint to paving surface ratio is much higher than with flags, often therefore the joints are often filled with a mortar slurry, though there are now pourable mortar or resin-based compounds to make life easier.

LAYING BRICKS ON A GRIT MORTAR BED

This method is much the same for block paving and setts laid on grit sand, replace the screed of mortar with sand.

Step 1 Create a supporting edge on one side using the same brick. Lay a 2.5 cm (1 in) bed of mortar or concrete about 10 cm (4 in) from the edge of the prepared foundations, place the brick on the mortar and tap it down. Build up some mortar or concrete against the outside edge of the brick to form the haunching, this should finish about an inch or so from the top of the edging and slope away from the paving. Smooth the surface with a trowel. Leave the kerb to cure overnight before continuing.

Step 2 Spread a layer of mortar 3–5 cm (1¼–2 in) thick on the compacted scalpings inside the newly laid edging. Use a piece of timber to get a smooth level surface by moving it backwards and forwards across the sand. For large areas a compactor could be used very briefly, as the sand should not be fully compacted.

Step 3 The bricks are placed neatly on the mortar, packed as closely together as possible. Designing the pattern so no bricks have to be cut has a real advantage for those new to paving but some designs, like herringbone, will inevitably require a half brick. Experts break bricks by striking them with a trowel, others can use a disc cutter! Once the path is finished, add the other edge in the same way as in step 1.

Step 4 Once the paving is finished brush kiln dried sand into the cracks between the bricks to pack them together.

SPOT FOR A BENCH

1

2

Step 1 Mark out an area just a little larger than your bench. Use a builder's square to check the corners are 90° (see marking out, above). If you can, tailor the size of the area to the size of your paving to avoid cutting.

Step 2 Dig out to the correct depth to allow for the sub-base, bedding and material. See the table above. If the paving is in turf make the finished level just below the turf for easy mowing.

Step 3 Spread a layer of scalping across the site and compact with a vibrating plate.

Step 4 Starting in one corner create a bed of mortar.

Step 5 Using a trowel make ridges in the mortar.

Step 6 Tap the first stone into position and, using a spirit level, check it is level.

Step 7 Repeat the process with the second stone and continue until the area is complete.

Step 8 Holding the mortar on a large trowel, move a little at a time into the joints. Pack mortar into the joints using the side of a small trowel. Use a pointing iron, or a length of hose to smooth the joints.

Step 9 After an hour or so sweep across the surface to remove any loose mortar.

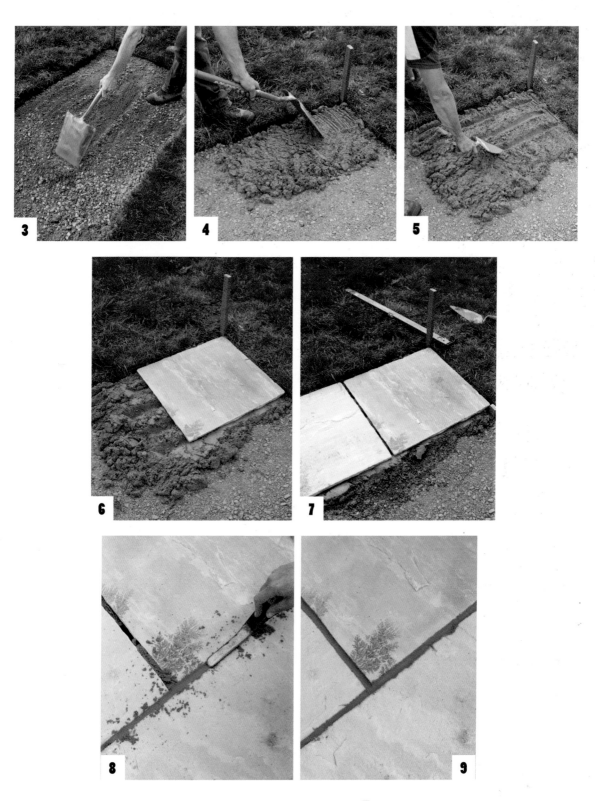

STEPPING STONES

Whether they are stone, mosaic, glass or wood, all stepping stones are installed in much the same way. The process is quick and simple requiring no special skills at all, which is why they are the perfect quick fix for providing a practical, durable path or just embellishing the garden floor. The material you select will depend on your aims, but as these are a low-cost, low-effort affair you can afford to be adventurous. Smooth stone or concrete slabs are durable and practical, mosaic-encrusted stones add a burst of colour and pattern to the garden floor, wood might sit better in some schemes but even bold hand-painted concrete slabs can be used, really putting your own stamp on the garden.

Set low in the grass, stepping stones can be mown over making maintenance simple and keeping edges neat. Paths with two very different characters intersect here, shaping the garden floor and creating a space for a sculpture.

1   2   3

STEPPING STONES

These stepping stones are hunks of oak 5 cm (2 in) thick and 25 cm (10 in) wide sawn from a large plank. The only embellishment has been to plan off the edges. The method below applies to all stepping stones set in turf.

Step 1 Lay out all the stepping stones. Adjust them so the form a pleasing line and so they are equally spaced at a distance which allows a comfortable gait as they are walked upon. Obviously the natural stride length of individuals varies considerably; the stones need to be arranged so most people can adjust their stride to fit. Leave all the stones in position and work on one step at a time. Using a spade, chop around the edge of the stone. Move the stone away and dig out the turf, creating a flat bottomed hole just one or two centimetres deeper than the stone. If you have a good lawn it may be possible to use an old bread knife to saw through the turf around the stone and prize the turf up using a fork.

Step 2 Put a layer of sharp sand in the base of the hole, just a little deeper than is needed to bring the stone up to just below the level of the turf. If it far easier to maintain a lawn if stepping stones are set so they can be simply mown over.

Step 3 Pace the stone into the hole and check it is level and sitting at the right height. You could use a spirit level but judging by eye and standing on it with both feet and testing if it rocks is normally accurate enough. If it does move bolster it up with more sand or remove some sand as needed. If there are spaces around the stone pack them with soil. Once you have done one stepping stone, the rest are far easier to get right first time. Bed in the remaining stones one at a time.

PEBBLE PATIO

Pebble patios are quite special because they are inherently part art, part paving. There is the option to stick to something plain or copy a pattern but there are so many possibilities in the materials which can be used and range of designs which can be created, planning a pebble patio is a feast for the imagination. Even simply varying the orientation of the pebbles to form a pattern can have a striking effect.

Despite the impressive results pebble mosaics are simple to create. The base is constructed in the same way as flags, a temporary or permanent restraining edge is needed, the permanent edge could be anything which will act as a kerb and works with the design (see section above on how to construct a kerb). A temporary edge might be formed by a framework of timber which can be removed once the surface is finished, or timber frames can be used to generate a regular design. For example a chequer board effect is far more easily achieved if you use a square timber frame template as guide. If the pattern includes a grid or areas defined by a particular material then these can be laid first and then the spaces filled in.

The pebble surface is built by spreading a small area of mortar on the compacted hardcore base so it is about 2.5 cm (1 in) to 3 cm (1¼ in) thick. The pebbles are then pushed into the mortar to about half their depth, the pebbles should be packed together as tightly as possible. When a reasonably sized area has been completed but before the mortar cures place a wide plank on the surface and tap it down gently to level the surface. Next day or when the mortar has cured slightly, brush a dry mix of 1:3 mortar into the gaps between the pebbles, do not over fill the joints or the surface loses part of its charm. Ensure the surface is bone dry before you begin or the mortar may stain the stones. When the surface is free of mortar water gently with a watering can.

A small area of pebble mosaic is an effective method of embellishing a paved surface.

Maintenance

The maintenance-free garden does not exist. Even one completely covered with paving has to be swept if is not to be colonized by a jungle of weeds. In some respects your gardening style will dictate how you maintain your paving from day to day. While some gardeners may welcome the softening effects of lush moss along paving joints, others will not. Longer term repairs and maintenance are vital to keeping the surface sound, though well laid paving should require little repair work. To prolong the life of the patio any small repairs required should be effected hastily.

The mossy carpet on these steps contributes greatly to their character.

WEEDS

Weeds can pop up in almost any paving, some plants will easily root in just a few millimetres of detritus which can build up on the paved surface and grow in these seemingly inhospitable circumstances. The easiest way to keep weeds from colonizing your paved garden floor is to sweep it regularly to stop detritus building up in the joints. Once they gain a foothold weeds grow, it seems, impossibly quickly. The larger they grow the further their roots extend into sand-filled joints and the more sand is removed as you yank the weeds out. Removing weeds while they are small is easier and causes less damage. If things really get out of hand then there are weed killers specifically designed for use on paving.

PRESSURE WASHING

Sweeping removes most loose dirt but once a year, normally in spring, some paving really benefits by being smartened up with a pressure washer. This washes away ingrained dirt and will get rid of algae built up through the winter leaving the paving looking fresh and nearly new. On paving with sand joints the force of the water can wash out the sand so it is important to keep the jet of water at a low angle, rather than blasting the water directly at the floor.

SEALANTS

Though in most cases there is no imperative to seal paving, there are a number of sealants on the market designed to protect hard garden surfaces from staining, growth of algae and the effects of the weather. Many products are formulated to work with a particular type of stone, brick or paviour. Sealants fall into two categories, surface coatings and impregnators. Coatings form skin on the surface of the paving to protect it, unfortunately this coating will eventually wear away to leave a patchy finish so the product has to be reapplied regularly. After many applications the finish can look a little shiny. Impregnators actually penetrate the body of the stone and offer a more permanent protection. Some products are sold as colour enhancers, the colours of the stone become far richer, similar to when it is wet. If you decide to seal your paving choose the product carefully and follow the manufacturer's instructions. Test any sealant it on a spare stone to ensure you like the finish as once applied the stone may well be changed permanently.

SAND JOINTS IN BUTT JOINTED PAVING

In the first three months or so it may be necessary to top up the level of sand in the joints as it settles. After a few months the joints should become stable.

GRAVEL

Though easy to lay, loose gravel is one of the harder surfaces to maintain as leaves and debris cannot be swept away. They have to be collected by hand or raked up. In the autumn a garden blower is handy to waft fallen leaves into an easily picked up heap. Left uncollected they will form a mulch which, when combined with the gravel, is the perfect situation for weed seeds to take root. Even with good maintenance, overtime small bits and pieces of detritus filter through the gravel and create a perfect seed bed under the stones. Weeding can be done with a quick shuffle of the hoe when seedlings are small; more established weeds have to be removed by hand. If there are no cultivated plants in the gravel weed killer is an option.

As gravel tends to travel and shift around, especially in areas with lots of foot fall, it becomes patchy, a rake can be used to take out ruts. A certain amount of gravel is also 'lost' so the gravel can be topped up when needed. A new layer of stones really freshens up the surface.

REPAIR

If stones or blocks begin to rock, hopefully it is a rogue stone that was not bedded quite as well as it should have been. However it could be the result of larger scale movement. The stone should be lifted and the old bedding and pointing removed and the stone replaced on a good bed. Damaged or missing pointing should be replaced as quickly as possible to prevent further damage by water penetrating the surface. Rake out all the loose or damaged pointing and re point the joint. It is worth making an effort to get a good match on the pointing, remembering the colour will change once it cures.

PAVING TO INSPIRE

A family terrace

Designed for relaxed cooking, eating and sitting back and enjoying the sun, this terrace lies directly outside a large kitchen and through the summer months the French doors are flung wide all day and the kitchen and paved outdoor area operate as one space. Everything in this area, from the furnishings to the choice of the paving, is solid and resilient. Designed for my own family, the 'built to last' character makes this carefree space ideal for a busy family with a host of teenagers.

Just a few months before this set of pictures was taken the ground level outside the kitchen was far higher and a small window looked out onto a retaining wall and planting at eye level. I decided to carve into the hill to open the kitchen onto the garden. About 600 tonnes of soil were swept away and French doors installed to produce a practical, sunny outdoor space and a vista to the boundary of the garden and beyond.

The paving is reclaimed York stone flags, a generic term for the many types of limestone stone quarried around Yorkshire in the north of England. These stones probably once served as floors in warehouses, factories or have been used as paths, worn smooth by years of pedestrian traffic. These stones are charmingly irregular and challenging to lay. They vary in thickness from 5–15 cm (2–6 in) and the largest is at least 7.5 × 10 cm (3 × 4 in). Even the smaller stones are heavy but the larger stones take several men to carry them. The irregular sizes, no two stones are the same, produce an irregular pattern where joints have to eased or balanced to give the impression that they are even. The major difficulty is planning so the stones fit; they should not be cut as the edges are as uneven and worn smooth as the face of the stones and any new, sharp cuts simply spoil the effect.

So achieving a straight edge finish is difficult unless the cuts can be disguised up against a wall or bed. Here the problem has been solved by leaving the edges untidy, stones interlocking with gravel.

To create additional space the terrace has been extended with a gravel floor, this is both a practical and aesthetic decision, a paving floor covering this entire area may begin to look too dominant in the enclosed space, the adjoining gravel-covered space provides a welcome change of texture corresponding to a change in the way the space is used. A gravel clad area is also far quicker and far less expensive to construct, including a gravelled area within your paving scheme will make your budget go further.

A beautiful Indian kadai is the centrepiece of the gravelled expanse encircled by eight untreated, planed cubes of soft wood stools. The kadai once used to prepare street food at Indian festivals, can be used as a vast fire pit, at 1.8 m (6 ft) in diameter there is plenty of space to get a good blaze going and the chunky stools are ideal for perching on to enjoy the warmth, or toast marshmallows. The kadai also has an enormous set of grills, charcoal rather than wood can be burnt and it becomes an excellent barbecue, large enough for any party. The stools make a handy place to stash food and utensils.

The planting and pots on this patio are very simple and unfussy. Large pieces of topiary are used to create drama and height, while the crimson-leaved acer 'Garnet' and orange gerberas and diascia pick up on the rusty tones of the kadai. At the end of the patio two large-bellied, squat pots are so full of character they are often left unplanted, sentinels at the edge of the space. Here they are the temporary home for *astelia* 'Westmorland' with a bronzy, metallic sheen that fits the planting colour scheme.

A string of striking objects lead the eye from the patio, across the lawns, through the vegetable and fruit gardens, to the countryside beyond so, though enclosed by a high bank on one side, this outdoor room feels open and spacious. The bank itself is strimmed infrequently through the summer to keep plants reasonably tidy whilst allowing wild flowers to seed and flourish attracting a host of bees and colourful butterflies. This casual approach to maintaining the bank gives it a softer look than barren shorn turf, encourages biodiversity and makes the space far more interesting as its colour and character changes through the seasons. The colonization of the bank has been a natural process so the plants are perfectly suited to the location, over time the population will undoubtedly change, but these pioneers are performing a valuable role stabilizing the surface of the bank.

The higher levels of the garden are reached by steps, thick slabs of oak projecting from the bank. A significant amount of metalwork is hidden in the bank to support the cantilevered steps. A steel beam or RSJ with plates welded to it runs up inside the bank, the oak steps are bolted to the metal and the whole structure is hidden so just the miraculous steps are on show.

The zen garden

Created using many elements of the minimal style of Japanese garden design, Eric Borja has designed this breathtaking garden around his home in France. Clipped and cloud-shaped trees combine with carefully orchestrated rock and gravel to make a garden with a clear Japanese style that sits comfortably around a very French building. Traditional Japanese gardens contain symbolism related to Buddhist and Shinto beliefs but, inspired by a visit to Japan, Borja uses elements and the essence of the Japanese garden to create his own.

In the Japanese tradition reduced scale and borrowed view are important elements alongside symbolism, where rocks and boulders are mountains or islands and gravel seas, rivers and ponds. The paving in this garden is inspirational, though its character is fundamental to developing the central theme in the garden the way materials have been combined, the rich patterns and textures which have been wrought with natural materials provide encouragement and ideas for those wanting to create beautiful paving with individuality and character in any garden. The paths look natural and artless yet clearly an enormous amount of skill, thought and design work has gone into their creation.

Around the house worn stone stepping-stones or *tobi ishi* sit in a flow of grey pebbles, wonderfully sculptural, this path needs a fair degree of care and thoughtfulness to traverse it successfully. Elsewhere in the garden flatter stones lie flat amongst flat pebbles to produce a more practical, though narrow, path, while in another area similar flat stones are set amongst the lush green of low growing plants. As one moves around the garden a rich variety of wonderfully textured paving marks out the route.

Though it cannot really be regarded as a practical part of the garden, immaculate raked gravel forms a large part of this garden floor, punctured by island rocks and small plants the fascinating, perfectly formed combed circles and sweeping curves in the gravel are a feast for the eyes. Not intended for foot traffic this set piece is there simply to be gazed upon. The best way to choose gravel is to look at samples where the gravel is to be spread amongst the plants and rocks it will share the area with. Look at the gravels in different lights and at different times of the day and then decide.

A gravel garden

When faced with the two patches of garden around his newly converted stone barn, photographer Clive Nichols took his cue from the building and the landscape around him. Like the barn itself the paving, edging and monolithic benches are quite literally hewn from the local hills. The local stone is Hornton, a limestone with a distinctive rich rusty brown colour.

This tawny stone is used with a creamy gravel to pave a large portion of the garden floor. Selecting just the right gravel, one to work with the richly coloured Hornton stone and provide the perfect foil for planting, took a great deal of thought. The garden has two separate areas: the first court yard garden at just 7 × 5 m (22 × 16 ft) is dedicated to outdoor dining and the other larger garden is about 25 × 25 m (72 × 72 ft).

Aesthetic, practical and economic factors all influenced the choice of gravel. The intention was to create an informal space where loose drifts of planting could be left to reinvent themselves anew each year, with serendipitous combinations of self seeded plants supplying the beds with new vigour. Now plants like the umbellifera angelica gigas, verbena bonariensis and dianthus carthusianorum are spilling from the original planting areas, colonising areas of gravel.

Punctuating the gravel with hunks of the natural stone spices up the garden floor. In one area hefty tranches of stone sawn from the same lump of rock are laid like random paving, the gravel seeping through the joints. In the larger garden natural rocks turned up in the soil are used to define the edge of the planting area. While huge slabs of Hornton stone cut from the local quarry and left unshaped are arranged to form a relaxed seating area around a gazing pool at the heart of the larger garden.

In the courtyard garden the gravel is simply laid on a weed suppressing membrane so plants can be planted straight into the gravel, whereas in the larger garden areas of soil edged with stone sweep around the edge of the garden and a bed of compacted scalping was put down before spreading the gravel.

Though compact the courtyard has a huge fountain set against a vivid painted rendered wall filling the garden with sound. The drama they create in the garden belies the simple lined brick and render construction. The colour of the wall, a deep red like the vibrant colours of the flowering plants and the exact shade of the gravel was chosen to work when set against the distinctively coloured local stone, the starting point for the entire garden.

An urban garden

Designed by Charlotte Rowe for a couple wanting a space for entertaining, this garden presented the designer with a number of difficulties which clever design strategies have solved so elegantly, they have become invisible.

The small garden has a main road at its end, has a good deal of shade, while the portion nearest the house is built over a basement office and gym.

The privacy and noise difficulties were addressed by locating a useful, green roofed bicycle shed behind a slatted cedar screen at the end of the garden, giving the garden a double skin. The feeling of seclusion is completed by a similar wooden screen, softened with climbing plants, around the whole garden. While the skylights used to allow light to the rooms below the garden are an integral part of the garden floor, rectangular slabs of glass which lead the eye into the garden which can be illuminated at night.

The garden is not large but by dividing it into distinct areas using the paving design it is made to appear more spacious. Making the space bright and light, the garden floor is for the most part made of a pale Portuguese limestone while contrasting strips of glossy black pebbles neatly cut the limestone floor into panels giving the floor character and defining the areas of the garden making it seem larger. One of the pebble-filled gullies has cleverly been used to disguise a drain. The size of the limestone flags has been carefully selected to fit the layout.

A monochrome theme and a limited palette of materials are skilfully manipulated to produce a coherent, smart space. A striking black polished concrete counter with a built in stainless steel barbecue provides a place to prepare and cook food as well as a place to perch and eat. In this area the limestone paving has been used to clad a wide L-shaped banquet while the polished concrete is used to form the back of the bench and a side table. The area is softened by troughs of fragrant lavender. A pair of comfortable garden sofas shaded by a large cantilevered parasol occupies the next area which is softened by mounds of verdant, shade loving plants.

A formal country garden

This wonderful formal country garden designed by Arne Maynard shows just how impressive two simple paving materials become when adroitly balanced; brick and gravel are skilfully combined to create a system of paths linking the various compartments of this garden and drawing the eye to the many remarkable features the garden holds and on into the countryside beyond.

A parterre, potager, elegant pool are criss-crossed by a network of paths either of brick or gravel or gravel punctuated by areas of brick or perhaps brick punctuated by areas of gravel. Neither material dominates and the overall effect is to provide far more interest and a richer texture than either material could produce alone. Each material flies solo at times: the pool edged with a sharp hedge of clipped box is given a further frame of pale gravel, giving it definition against the green of the grass while a practical path of solid brick leads to the back door. On the whole, however, the garden floor is the work of a duo of materials which go a long way to defining the character of the garden and giving the garden a unity.

The paths are lined with a profusion of fragrant lavender which lolls on the paths, softening their edges and releasing a burst of scent as they are brushed past as well as well-established, clipped box hedges. The paths encourage a fairly leisurely pace, for although they are poker-straight as is required by such a formal design, they are reasonably wide and the paving has no directional pull. The loose gravel has a random, shifting surface while the bricks are laid in a basket weave pattern which has no direction. So although the paths afford passage through the garden, create wonderful vistas and have the ample reward of magnificent mirrored stainless steel obelisks, armillary spheres and the Sentinel, mirrored stainless steel water feature (all by David Harber) at their end or along their length, there is no hurry, the paths, like the lavender, encourage a relaxed pace.

A Provençal garden

Covering a 20 acres (8 hectares) this garden is a luxury, but the use of paving is inspirational with plenty ideas to borrow, adapt and fire the imagination.

Once a wheat field this vast garden is divided into compartments defined by hedges, rose-covered arches, cypress trees and tunnels of trained trees but it is the many paths that link the garden, guiding the visitor from one room to the next. Bricks, terracotta tiles, smooth pebbles, loose gravel and stone flags are all used to concoct surfaces with amazing texture and personality. The idea of the limited palette is cast aside as the paths move from garden room to garden room over the vast area.

Stretched along the back of the house a terrace clothed in fine gravel is probably the plainest surface in the garden but to compensate it is sprinkled with plenty of furniture informal groupings, tables, chairs, benches, and splendid pots all under the cool shade of the stately plane trees – the perfect space for leisurely dining. One of which is fitted with a staircase spiralling up its trunk to a tree platform above affording a bird's eye view of the garden spread below.

In contrast to the terrace the rest of the paving in the garden is a melange of materials artfully used to form paths and paving to fit their location. Strong paths with a repeating pattern of brick frames packed with smooth dark pebbles are flanked by equally strong

clipped hedges and bowl through lawns strewn with topiary and straddle a brick edged rill. While a softer, earthy combination of terracotta tiles and pale terracotta bricks echo the antique terracotta vessel in a tightly clipped box jacket they are ranged around. Even the flags in the path to the door are not alone but embellished with smooth stones pushed into the extra wide mortar joints. Paths vary in width according to need but the narrowest shoots under an arcade of trained trees. Barely wide enough to walk along this thin slice of bricks takes concentration and care to travel, but its narrow gauge in contrast encourages haste. From the end of the arcade the eye quickly skims to the path's conclusion. It is almost more of a sculptural device than path.

An artist's garden

Bold and brilliant, the lavish use of
dazzling colours by the artist Keeyla
Meadows in her garden extends to all
aspects of the garden, including paving.

Ceramics, furniture, plants and paving are all a part of the confident schemes which vibrate with colour. Even where run of the mill paving is used materials are imaginatively combined to make surfaces brimming with character and energy.

Though packed with colourful pots, benches and sculptures as the planting is abundant and informal the garden retains a natural, organic character. Often mundane paving surfaces are studded with coloured ceramic tiles produced by the artist. A path of brick which seems to meander around random slabs of stone like water around obstacles is peppered with blue ceramic tiles, resembling flotsam on the river of brick. An area of paving in front of a water sculpture reflects the colour of the piece in a chequer board of yellow ceramic tiles and brick.

In another part of the garden hexagonal sett-like tiles, each baring a colourful crescent moon, snake through planted areas and alongside a ceramic sculpture set in the ground towards a magnificent ceramic pot. This inspirational, uninhibited garden, with its extreme use of colour may be too brave for some but clearly demonstrates that paving can be the vehicle for great creativity, not just a neutral, practical foil for the rest of the garden.

In a small space every centimetre has to be hard-working. This vivacious, playful design by Ana Sanchez-Martin packs in a dining area, a spot for relaxing, an outdoor kitchen and its own fabulous work of art.

The lively garden floor employs two types of paving and a slice of decking to create an interesting layout in the small space. The hardwood decking, furnished with enormously plump bean bag chairs, is reserved for complete relaxation.

Two large circles of pale York stone are set in a sea of smooth white pebbles to make a continuous floor. The pale colour keeps the garden bright and light and the change in texture is enough to clearly define the areas without over-complicating the scheme with a paving in a contrasting colour. The bespoke York stone circles of three concentric rings of stones have been coated with an impregnating treatment to preserve their fresh good looks. The pebbles are not a true pebble mosaic, they come in the form of tiles fixed to a backing mesh. This can be cut to size and fixed like other paving, taking care that the jointing does not ruin the individual shape of the pebbles.

A glossy wirework table and chairs occupies one circle and so its position is fixed within the design and the dining area clearly delineated. Using the airy wirework furniture for the small space is a skilful choice, its ornate black coloured framework ensures it is seen yet it has no bulk and the garden can be seen through it, so it seems to occupy little space.

The lush green planting is contained within a two-tier raised bed which flows around the circles of paving. The flowing lines of the garden are incredibly

A small urban garden

successful in detracting from its boxy shape. The walls of the raised bed are rendered and fitted with a comfortable hardwood bench top, perfect for extra seating. To the side of the garden a neat outdoor kitchen complete with cupboards and preparation space means the cook does not have to be marooned inside while drinks are being enjoyed outside. An integrated gas barbecue is flanked by the same York stone used on the floor to form the work surface. The star of the garden which gives it masses of personality is the lively mosaic of glass tesserae. Designed especially for this project, a collaboration between the designer and mosaic artist Celia

Gregory the stylized leaves and snaking river of tiles adorning the end wall of the garden with an uplifting burst of colour all year round. The wall also houses a slice of green wall, providing more plant space without taking up valuable floor area. This lofty end wall could be oppressive but decorated and planted it provides an uplifting outlook from the house.

Designed by Ana Sanchez-Martin for clients with a young family who wanted an original, colourful, funky garden for entertaining this happy, sparkling, lively space certainly fits the brief.

Index

Page numbers in *italic* refer to illustrations.

Acknowledgements

A huge thank you to Clive Nichols for his remarkable photography and for putting up with me once again on this, our ninth book. My thanks to all the garden owners and designers whose splendid gardens feature in this book – with special thanks to Ana Sanchez (A Small Town Garden) and Charlotte Rowe (An Urban Garden), for generously discussing their designs with me.

My gratitude to Stuart Mansbridge, Roderick McLean, Jon Hobson and Ben Aston who, with Herculean strength, built The Family Terrace from vast slabs of York stone and to Stuart for his building expertise on shoot days.

Thank you to Emma Bastow and all those involved with this project at New Holland.

Finally, my love and thanks to Harriet, Nancy, Joshua and David for cheerfully putting up with it all, once again.

Contact Clare or follow her garden blog at **ClareMatthews.com**